R. D. Bartlett and Pa

Geckos

Everything About Housing, Health, Nutrition, and Breeding

Filled with Full-color Photographs and Illustrations

BARRON'S

2 CONTENTS

Geckos are lizards most commonly found in subtropical and tropical regions. They share, to a greater or lesser degree, the following characteristics: a retiring demeanor; nocturnal activity patterns; and many have expanded toe pads, which give these lizards the ability to climb walls, to cling to vertical rock faces, or to "hug" tree trunks or branches. All except the eublepharines have no eyelids (the eyes are protected by a clear scale). They range in color from a subdued gray-brown to a bright kelly green, and in pattern from strongly banded and spotted to unicolored.

Gecko Families

Geckos belong to the infraorder Gekkota, a grouping that, depending on the authority followed, includes either three or five lizard families. The most liberal accounting delineates the families of the Gekkota as:

- Eublepharidae: The eyelid geckos
- Gekkonidae: The typical geckos
- Dibamidae: The dibamid lizards
- Xantusiidae: The night lizards
- Pygopodidae: The Australian and New Guinean footless lizards.

The more conservative accounting of the infraorder Gekkota discounts the xantusids as members and continues to consider the euble-

A peacock day gecko at home.

pharine geckos as a subfamily, rather than as a full family.

Depending on whether you follow the conservative or liberal track, the gecko families can be divided as follows:

Conservative
- Family Gekkonidae
- Subfamily Eublepharinae
- Subfamily Gekkoninae
- Subfamily Sphaerodactylinae

Liberal
- Family Eublepharidae
- Family Gekkonidae
- Subfamily Gekkoninae
- Subfamily Diplodactylinae
- Subfamily Sphaerodactylinae

The main difference between the two classification delineations relates to the eublepharines—

the leopard, banded, and fat-tailed geckos. The eublepharines are the only geckos to have functional eyelids. Also, all eublepharines lack toe pads and all lay soft-shelled eggs. Like many other geckos, eublepharines also have a voice.

The Subfamilies

Gekkoninae geckos lack eyelids and usually produce two hard-shelled eggs per clutch. They may or may not have toe pads. These geckos can vocalize. Examples are the tokay and day geckos.

Diplodactyline geckos lack eyelids but produce paired soft-shelled eggs. These species vocalize. Examples are the velvet and New Caledonian geckos as well as the Australian genus *Diplodactylus*. The toe pads may vary; some are well developed, others are absent.

Sphaerodactylines lack eyelids and produce only a single egg per clutch. These are the tiny New World geckos; none can vocalize. Reef and ashy geckos are examples. Some species have prominent toe pads; others lack them.

The short-snouted giant gecko, **Rhacodactylus chahoua,** *is only now becoming popular.*

Where Are Geckos Found?

Geckos are well represented in the warmer climes of both the Old and New Worlds. With the help of human commerce, many gecko species have colonized areas of the world far from their homelands.

The 700-plus species of geckos occur on islands and continents. They may be found in sandy deserts, arid savannas, rocky steppes, areas of tidal wrack, tropical rain forests, and mountaintop cloud forests. They occur in suitable habitats from areas below sea level to elevations of nearly 2.5 miles (4 km).

What's in a Name?

Much is in a name, for it is by their names that we are able to identify and discuss the various organisms that share our world.

Holodactylus africanus, the African clawed gecko, is so nocturnal that it is difficult to induce it to open its eyes in bright light.

To systematists it is the "formal name," the name given at the time an organism is officially (scientifically) described, that is the most important. This is a standardized name, which is applicable only to a single given species. As additional information is gathered, the original name given the organism might change, but these changes are made in a set and methodical manner. The changes and the reasons for them are published and any systematist who chooses can remain up to date and in sync.

Common Name

On the other hand, the other set of names—the common names—are often arbitrary. Let's use a bird for an example. The American robin, a thrush, was named because it reminded the English colonists of the European robin, a very different bird.

Thus the name "robin" applies to two different birds.

However, the scientific designations *Turdus migratorius* for the American bird and *Erithacus rubicola* for the European one are different. Each applies to only the single species. There can be no confusion about which species one is discussing when the scientific designation is used. This holds true for reptiles, and by extension, to geckos as well.

To many folks, a gecko—any gecko—seen on a house is a "house gecko." And there are a lot of geckos, a lot of very different geckos, that are seen either regularly or infrequently on houses. However, if the term house gecko is mentioned to a herpetologist, he or she will immediately ask "what kind?" If the answer is *"Hemidactylus turcicus,"* there will be no confusion.

So it's best to begin learning and using scientific names. Doing so will enable you to discuss your hobby with others, all of you secure in the knowledge that you are speaking about the same species.

UNDERSTANDING GECKOS

*Most geckos are nocturnal, but a few species are diurnal. These day-active types include some of the most brilliantly colored members of the family—among them the day geckos (**Phelsuma**). Geckos tend to be less active when the wind is blowing strongly or when the weather cools. House and wall geckos can often be seen around porch lights feeding on the insects drawn to the illumination. They may also bask in the warmth of the bulbs on cool evenings.*

As captives, geckos need warm temperatures (variable by species); live foods and/or fruit-honey diets (variable by species); desert, woodland, rain forest, or savanna terrariums (also variable by species). The techniques for providing water and lighting to geckos also vary—by gecko species, of course. In general, terrestrial geckos will often lap water from a dish or lap droplets from freshly misted substrate, whereas, until acclimated, arboreal species often insist on drinking pendulous droplets from elevated positions such as leaves and limbs (see page 23).

Life Span

How long your gecko will live is very much an open-ended question. The life span of a captive

The eyes of the giant leaf-tailed gecko,
Uroplatus fimbriatus, *are intricately patterned.*

gecko will depend upon numerous variables, which can be reduced to two factors—the condition of the gecko when you received it (what was its age and health?) and the sort of care you give the lizard (is its life under your care better than it would have been in the wild?).

If properly cared for, even some of the smaller species can live upward of five years. For example, tiny yellow-tailed geckos (*Sphaerodactylus nigropunctatus flavicauda*), all adult when received, survive for more than six years as captives. Imported adult Bibron's geckos (*Pachydactylus bibroni*) regularly exceed a decade as captives and a pair of Standing's day geckos, *Phelsuma standingi*, again fully adult when imported from Madagascar, can live for more than 15 years.

Size

The vast majority of the world's gecko species are between 4 and 7 inches (10.2–17.8 cm) in

TIP

Comparative Sizes of the Largest and Smallest Geckos

Rhacodactylus leachianus is almost 10 times the length and 100+ times the bulk of *Lepidoblepharis sanctaemartae*!

overall length—and about half that length is the tail. There are, of course, species on both sides of that size range. Let's consider the extremes.

The largest: The largest gecko species yet known was designated as *Hoplodactylus delacourti*. Probably extinct, the single stuffed specimen of this hulking lizard measures 24.5 inches (62 cm) in overall length. Its point of origin is unknown, but because other members of the genus occur on New Zealand it is speculated that *H. delacourti* is from that geographic region.

At 14.5 inches (36.8 cm) from nose to tail tip, the New Caledonian giant gecko (*Rhacodactylus leachianus*) is thought to be the world's largest

living gecko. Other geckos approach or attain 1 foot (30.5 cm) in length.

Among these are

✔ Standing's day gecko (*Phelsuma standingi*) of Madagascar

✔ Giant day gecko (*Phelsuma madagascariensis grandis*) of Madagascar

✔ Tokay gecko (*Gekko gecko*) of tropical Asia (and Florida!)

✔ Green-eyed gecko (*Gekko smithi*) of Southeast Asia

✔ Giant bent-toed gecko (*Cyrtodactylus biordinus*) of the Solomon Islands

The smallest: The smallest geckos are the members of a New World subfamily, the Sphaerodactylinae. Of these, *Lepidoblepharis sanctaemartae* is the smallest, attaining a mere 1.5 inches (3.8 cm) in total length. Many of the reef and ashy geckos (genus *Sphaerodactylus*) are nearly as small, topping out at 2 to 3 inches (5.1–7.6 cm) in total length.

Among the smallest of the Old World geckos are the 3-inch (7.6-cm) long members of the genus *Tropiocolotes*.

Physical Traits

The Gecko's Eyes

The eyes of many gecko species are wonders to behold! Those of many nocturnal species bear wonderfully colored and intricately veined irides (irises) and strangely shaped, often scalloped, pupils. Conversely, the eyes of many diurnal forms are less ornate, of a dark color, and have rather standard round pupils.

Gekko vittatus is often called the skunk gecko.

The green-eyed gecko, Gekko smithi, *is aptly named.*

The Mexican banded gecko, Coleonyx elegans, *occurs in both a striped and a banded phase.*

Without lids: The eyes of the members of the family Gekkonidae (typical geckos) have no functional lids. Instead, the lids have fused, and a large transparent scale, the brille or spectacle, permanently covers and protects the eye. The brille is cleaned frequently by the broad, flat tongue of the gecko. (This same procedure is used by the eublepharine species that have fully functional lids and no protective brille.)

With lids: The members of the gecko family Eublepharidae (meaning "with eyelids") have fully functional eyelids. The species include the leopard and banded geckos and allies, all often collectively called eyelid or eublepharine geckos.

TIP

Records of Interest

✔ A Seychelles skin-sloughing gecko (*Ailuronyx seychellensis*) was maintained for more than six years by the Chaffee Zoological Gardens in Fresno, California. When received by the zoo, it was a wild-collected adult.

✔ A male Namib sand gecko (*Chondrodactylus angulifer* ssp.) survived for almost 11 years at Woodland Park Zoo in Seattle.

✔ Mexican banded geckos (*Coleonyx e. elegans*) received as wild-collected adults have lived for more than 12 years as captives at both the Houston Zoological Gardens in Texas and in my collection.

✔ The somewhat smaller Tucson banded gecko (*C. variegatus bogerti*) has exceeded 15 years as a captive.

✔ Several records exist of leopard geckos (*Eublepharis macularius*) having lived for more than 20 years as captives. A similar life span is noted for numerous tokay geckos (*Gekko gecko*).

✔ Besides the Standing's day gecko, several congenerics have survived captivity for more than a decade. Among these are a Seychelles giant day gecko (*P. sundbergi*) in a private collection and a Round Island day gecko (*P. guentheri*) that was maintained by the Jersey Wildlife Preservation Trust in England.

✔ Even the greater frog-eyed gecko (*Teratoscincus scincus*), often thought of as a difficult captive, has survived in captivity for more than 12 years at the Fort Worth Zoo in Texas.

Note the diversity of color of these hatchling leopard geckos.

The pupils: The vertically elliptical pupils of the nocturnal geckos are remarkable in their diversity of shape. The pupils of the banded geckos are gently curved, those of the tokay have four gently curving scallops, and those of the giant Madagascan leaf-tailed gecko have more accentuated scallops. When tightly contracted in bright light, the pupils appear as straight hairline slits, undulating waves that are equally thin, or as a series of two, three, or four pinpoints. The tight closure of the vertical pupil probably protects the light-sensitive retina of nocturnal forms from the sunlight as well as reducing glare, thus enhancing daylight vision. These would both be valid concerns for species that are wonderfully adapted for life in reduced-light situations.

The day and Old World dwarf geckos (genera *Phelsuma* and *Lygodactylus*), which are active by day, have round pupils that do not contract as tightly as those of the nocturnal species. Round pupils are also the hallmark of the diurnal and crepuscular yellow-headed geckos (and relatives) of the genus *Gonatodes*. However (and uncharacteristically), round pupils also are to be found in the tiny reef and ashy geckos as well as conspecifics of the genus *Sphaerodactylus*, which are at least partially nocturnal.

At least as interesting as the pupils are the colors and venation in the irides of many nocturnal gecko species. Often the eye color is indistinguishable from the skin color. The patterns in the eye are so intricate that the lidless eyes of many species blend almost imperceptibly into the head as well as into background for which the gecko is best adapted (*Rhacodactylus* sp.). Others stand out in stark relief (*Palmatogecko rangei*). Golds, oranges, greens, and reds are the colors most frequently seen in geckos' eyes.

Eye structure: Rods and cones are abundant in the retina of many geckos. The abundance of these structures enhances both sight and color perception in both reduced- and strong-light situations. The retina also contains an abundance of nerve cells and fibers. Some gecko species lack the cones, having the retina packed with rods instead. These species have wonderfully acute sight in the darkness but no color perception.

The Gecko's Toes

Form follows function: The feet and toes of geckos are as varied as the purposes for which they have evolved. The webbed feet and expanded single digital pads of the flying geckos (*Ptychozoon* sp.) assist in both parachuting glides and secure climbing. The extensive webbing on the feet of the sand-adapted geckos, *Palmatogecko rangei* (a species of the southwest African fog-deserts that is commonly known as the web-footed gecko), lack the expanded climbing lamellae, but the webs serve admirably as snowshoes and enhance sand-swimming abilities. The toes of the sphere-toed geckos (genus *Sphaerodactylus*) terminate in a single rounded subdigital disk, whereas those of the leaf-toed geckos (genus *Phyllodactylus*) bear two expanded (leaflike) terminal subdigital pads. The house and turnip-tailed geckos (*Hemidactylus* and related genera, and *Thecadactylus*) bear a pair of elongated subdigital pads on each toe. The house geckos of the genus *Tarentola* have subdigital pads for the entire length of the toes.

Several gecko species lack all claws (*Crenadactylus ocellatus*, the clawless gecko) or some claws (*Chondrodactylus angulifer*, the South African sand gecko); several have retractile claws (the turnip-tailed gecko, *Thecadactylus rapicaudus*); others have the claws prominently fixed (flying geckos, *Ptychozoon* sp.). The bent-toed geckos (*Cyrtodactylus* and related genera) are aptly named. Lacking even vestiges of expanded disks, the toes when viewed laterally are seen to be kinked and strongly clawed. Even though lacking subdigital pads, these geckos are fast and agile climbers on rocks and trees. The common name of one species, the "lizard-fingered gecko" (genus *Saurodactylus*), is a literal translation of its genus name. This gecko has short toes that are not prominently kinked.

Some geckos lack both subdigital pads and kinks (the Caspian straight-fingered gecko, *Alsophylax pipiens*).

Many sand dwellers have combs or serrate scales fringing their toes, which help them in moving over the shifting terrain.

Subdigital pads: What, exactly, are the subdigital pads and how do they work? The pads are made up of rows of transverse layers or lamellae (singular, lamella). These lamellae either grow as a single piece across the width of the toe or are divided medially.

The lamellae contain tens of thousands of tiny hairlike structures called setae (singular, seta),

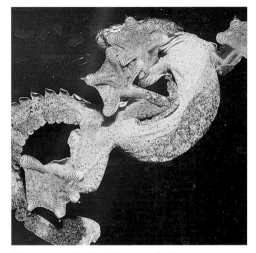

The camouflaging flanges of skin are readily visible (but not extended) on this flying gecko, Ptychozoon lionatum.

each of which divides and terminates in several hundred (often) watchglass-shaped spatulae (singular, spatula). It is the ability of these spatulae to fit into minute irregularities and create weak attractive forces that give a gecko its remarkable scansorial (climbing) abilities.

It is not necessary for the gecko to be alive for the spatulae to grasp tightly to their support.

What's in a Tail?

Some geckos will autotomize their tails with little more incentive than a mere brush by a keeper's or collector's hand or at the merest touch of a predator.

The autotomized tail wriggles convulsively, often drawing the attention of the attacker for a period of time sufficient to allow the now abbreviated lizard to escape. The tails then regenerate, but the regrown member often does not look at all like the original. Although the

An autotomized (broken) tail usually causes no inconvenience to a gecko. This is a crested gecko.

original tail is usually similar in scalation to the body and sleekly rounded, tapered, or flattened, regenerated tails may differ radically in scalation, and may be bulbous and ungainly. If the break is unclean or partial, one, two, or even three tails may regenerate.

Some gecko species have derived both their common and scientific names from the appear-

Regenerated tails (such as that of this fat-tailed gecko) often bear no resemblance to the original appendage.

ance of a regenerated tail. One such is the Latin American turnip-tailed gecko, *Thecadactylus rapicaudus.*

Tails have several functions other than autotomizing and affording the gecko a chance to escape.

✔ The platelike scales on the dorsal surface of the tail of the greater frog-eyed gecko (*Teratoscincus s. scincus*) scrape together and make audible rasping sounds.

✔ The tail of the flying geckos of the genus *Ptychozoon* lend stability during the lizards' gliding flights.

✔ The tails of both Australian and Madagascan leaf-tailed geckos (genera *Phyllurus* and *Uroplatus*) are so flattened that they help the lizards blend imperceptibly into their treetrunk backgrounds.

✔ The tailtip of the giant geckos (*Rhacodactylus*) bear clinging setae that help stabilize the lizards while climbing and are prehensile as well.

✔ The tails of leopard and fat-tailed geckos (*Eublepharis macularius* and *Hemitheconyx caudicinctus*) store fat in times of plenty. These reserves are then drawn on when prey is scarce or when weather conditions force inactivity.

✔ The attractively whorled original tails of eublepharines are wriggled to and fro as the lizard prepares to pounce on its prey; however, the heavy and unattractive regenerated tails usually are not flexible enough for wriggling.

✔ Some Australian diplodactyline geckos use their tails as burrow plugs.

✔ Other species of the same subfamily exude a sticky substance from specialized glands on the top of the tail; if the gecko is extremely distressed, this syrupy substance may be forcibly discharged over a distance of 1 foot (30.5 cm) or more.

✔ The tails of others (e.g., the New Zealand geckos of the genus *Naultinus*) are quite strongly prehensile.

Tail language and function: Thus, we see that the tails of geckos are as diverse as the creatures themselves, and that a tail is not necessarily merely a tail. It may be wagged to indicate an excitement level, or may be used as a stopper, as an aid in climbing, or for any number of other purposes. In all cases, their tails are another example of the remarkable adaptations of these lizards.

The Senses

Voice Implies Hearing

It would be counterproductive for a group of reptiles to be able to vocalize if others of their kind were not able to hear and respond to the sounds. Experimentation has shown that the hearing acuity of nocturnal geckos is well developed. The hearing ability of diurnal species may be somewhat less so.

Although many geckos of both the families Eublepharidae and Gekkonidae have voices, it would seem that all those of the subfamily Sphaerodactylinae are silent. The loud and frequent vocalizations of the Asian tokay (*Gekko gecko*) and the South African barking (also called "garrulous") geckos of the genus *Ptenopus* are well described. Other species click, squeak, squeal, chirp, or chuckle.

Although it is the males of most species that vocalize, the females of at least some species are also able to produce sounds. In general, it is the males that vocalize messages of territoriality and aggression as well as sexual interest.

A Boehme's giant day gecko cleans its face.

The Nose Knows

The sense of smell is also important to geckos. Not only do the paired Jacobson's organs inside the mouth seem to play a major role in scent identification, but geckos also seemingly nose around in an active effort to actually pick up telltale molecules. Watch your geckos explore their cage or a new territory. Often they pick specific sites to investigate, such as food dishes, egg-deposition sites, and cagemates. Nose to task, they also use their tongues in exploring.

The Gecko Tongue

As a group, geckos have well-developed, long, broad, motile tongues that are slightly notched at the tip. The tongue is extended frequently and is used in many ways. It carries particles of scent into contact with the openings of the paired Jacobson's organs in the anterior palate. There the scents are analyzed. The tongue is also used in tasting objects, mostly to identify them for possible consumption. A gecko's sense of taste seems well developed.

Captive day geckos, for instance, will consistently and preferentially choose the sweetest fruit-honey mixture to eat.

The tongue is also used to help determine the receptivity of potential breeding partners (by

carrying pheromones—species-specific chemical stimulants—to the mouth), to help in the finding of suitable egg-deposition sites, and to clean the nose and eyes.

The Skin and Scales

The protective skin: The skin of the gecko serves many functions, the most apparent of which is protection of the delicate inner being from the harshness of the environment.

The skin can also play a significant part in the defense of the gecko. Certainly, by its color and texture the skin plays a major role in blending the gecko with its background. But there is more to the skin of the gecko, both in structure and function, than meets the eye.

The outermost skin: The outer layer of the gecko's skin, the epidermis, is composed of a material called keratin. Every scale—be it of the tiny granular type in which the yellow-headed gecko is clad, the enlarged (fishlike) variety of the frog-eyed gecko, or the prominently tuberculate, almost spiny, scales of the odd little African rough-scaled gecko—is merely a modified section of epidermis. The specialized transparent eyecaps of geckos without eyelids are also composed of keratin. It is this outermost layer, the scaly covering, that is periodically shed and is the most noticeable to us. The process of skin-shedding is technically known as ecdysis. It is from this keratinous outer layer of skin that the gecko derives its dry scaly feel. Geckos may shed their skins almost entirely or in a patchwork manner. To rid themselves of the exfoliating skin shards they may rub themselves against twigs, rocks, or other solid material, scratch the skin off with their claws, or contort and pull it off with their jaws. Many gecko

species consume the skin as it is shed; other species do not.

The inner layer: Beneath the epidermis is the dermis. It is highly vascularized, contains connective tissue, bony, rigid plates called osteoderms, and pigment cells. Prismatic effects and the concentrations of the pigments within the cells at any given moment can be altered by nerve stimulation and/or hormonal activity. This accounts for both the perceived standard color as well as any color changes.

Structures in the skin: Although the skin of most lizards is largely free of glands, the femoral and preanal pores possessed by most gecko species and the secretion-expelling caudal (tail) glands of certain diplodactyline geckos are noteworthy exceptions.

The Endolymphatic (Chalk) Sacs

Certain species of geckos of the subfamily Gekkoninae bear a large chalk or endolymphatic sac on each side of the neck. Species of the genus *Phelsuma*, the day geckos of Madagascar, bear these sacs. Viewed from above, the sacs look like rounded bulges. Viewed from below, the white contents of calcium carbonate can usually be seen through the more translucent throat skin. The role of the sacs has not been determined, but there are several interesting theories.

Egg laying: The sacs are largest on the females, and are especially prominent during eggshell formation. It has been suggested that these calcium deposits are the main source for the eggshell material. This theory is lent credence by the facts that the sacs increase in size during the reproductive season and that only the members of the Gekkoninae, a subfamily that lays hard-shelled eggs, have the sacs.

Calcium metabolism: The fact that the males also possess the sacs detracts somewhat from the egg-laying theory. This suggests that the sacs are used in calcium metabolism.

Equilibrium: Another theory is that the sacs are static balance organs. This would help account for their presence in both sexes. Perhaps it will be found that their function embraces all of the current theories. In time, more will be known about the role(s) and value(s) of these organs.

Gecko Behavior in Captivity

Because of the several very different lifestyles embraced by the various geckos, it is difficult to generalize on the behavior of these lizards. For particulars see the discussions in the individual species accounts.

There are, however, a few generalizations that can be made.

✔ Although most female geckos will rather peacefully coexist with others of their own species and sex, sexually mature males of the same (or closely allied) species will fight savagely with others of their sex. Sexually mature geckos of all species are best housed in pairs or trios (one male and two females). Visual barriers (branches, hollow logs, hide boxes) in a cage (or even between cages) will be appreciated by all.

✔ Antagonism and unease between male geckos will be manifested by rapid head bobs and lateral nods. Pursuit and actual skirmishing will rapidly follow. Males in closely allied species groups (e.g., giant day and Standing's day geckos) will fight as persistently as males of the same species group.

The gular chalk (endolymphatic) sacs of this Standing's day gecko are easily seen.

✔ Head bobbing and nodding may also indicate courtship when used by a male in the presence of a female.

✔ Tail wagging and writhing may indicate nervousness (when used in the presence of geckos of the same sex), have sexual overtones (when used in the presence of geckos of the opposite sex), or indicate an interest in a prey item (when employed by a hungry, hunting gecko).

✔ Of the two gecko groups, the members of the eyelid geckos (leopard, fat-tailed) seem to resent handling less than most of the true geckos.

✔ The skin of all is easily torn but the skin of the day geckos and the skin-sloughing gecko is especially delicate. As a generality, geckos should be considered display lizards that should not be handled.

YOUR GECKO'S HOUSING NEEDS

A basic understanding of what a gecko needs in housing will go a long way toward helping you keep a pet gecko comfortable in captivity. Stated otherwise, simulating natural conditions will help promote natural behavior in a captive specimen.

Perhaps 150 species are rather regularly seen in the pet trade. To provide suitable captive conditions, you will need to correctly identify your gecko, then learn its adult size and habitat preferences.

Cages for arboreal gecko species should be vertically oriented; those for terrestrial species should be horizontally oriented. Although desert geckos prefer low humidity in the cage, the preference of most is not for absolute dryness. Tropical rain forest and woodland species require a higher overall humidity than desert and dry savanna forms (see pages 21–23).

What you provide in the way of decorative backdrop furniture in the terrarium may matter more to you than to the gecko. As long as your gecko has the perches, hiding areas, climbing surfaces, visual barriers, and temperatures it needs, it won't care what color scheme you choose.

Spider geckos, Agamura persica, seek refuge in rock crevices.

Terrariums

For arboreal geckos, the height of the terrarium provided should be of as much consideration as the floor space. The height of the cage is far less important if you are housing terrestrial geckos.

There are four types of terrariums that may be considered. All can have both terrestrial and arboreal applications.

Basic Caging

Whereas elaborately planted terrariums are the norm among European herpetoculturists, many American hobbyists prefer cages that are basic in both design and simplicity. Such basic caging can be adapted from premade aquariums (the all-glass types serve well in this capacity and are readily available in many sizes) or can be built (by handymen or cabinet makers) from wood and glass, or in some cases wood and wire.

Dimensions: When terrariums/cages are built, it is a good idea to incorporate large casters

This 15-gallon (56.7-L) terrarium contains several neon day geckos and ornate day geckos.

This is stapled in place on three sides, but can be rolled up and out of the way or removed from the top and south side (door side) if desired. A heat lamp is activated when necessary. To assure the comfort of the lizards, except for the removable front and top, the plastic sheeting can (and probably should) remain in place throughout the winter months. The geckos spend hours hanging on the sunny uprights of the frame or may leisurely bask on the horizontals of the door frame. The bottom can be left bare or a low frame can be installed that will retain a clean sand substrate. Potted plants (cycads or ficus) provide visual barriers and decoration.

These cages are ideal for breeding colonies of day geckos, tokays, and related species.

The actual dimensions of cages such as these can vary according to your individual needs but it is suggested that you never construct them so large that they cannot be easily rolled through both interior and exterior doors.

Using an Aquarium/Terrarium

The glass terrarium can be oriented in the standard (top-up) position for terrestrial gecko species, or positioned in an upright position for arboreal species. A suitable top (or front, as the case may be) will need to be provided.

With the standard orientation, this poses no problem. However, when the upright orientation is preferred, formulating an escape-proof front becomes more difficult. This may be approached from two angles.

First, if not too heavy, a glass front may be cut and held in position with a hinge of Silastic

into their design so that they may be easily moved about. This is especially handy when large terrariums/cages are involved.

In warm climates, where many gecko species can remain outdoors for most or all of the year, large step-in caging may be used for many arboreal species. Those having dimensions of 66 (height) × 48 (length) × 30 (width) inches (167.6 × 121.9 × 76.2 cm) will prove very satisfactory. The frames are made of 2 × 2 inch (5.1 × 5.1 cm) lumber, the base is from 0.75 inch (19 mm) marine plywood, and the wire is 0.125 inch (3.2 mm) mesh hardware cloth. The small mesh of the wire assures that all but the smallest feed crickets will remain within the cage. When placed on casters, the overall height is elevated to 71 inches (180.3 cm), which allows the cages to be rolled indoors (through sliding patio doors) if it does become necessary.

If left outdoors during cool weather, the cages are wrapped in clear 4 mil vinyl or polyethylene.

aquarium sealant. A hook and hasp may be similarly held in place on the opposite side. I have found that if the edge of the glass door rests flush against the table or stand top (or the inside glass of the terrarium), the sealant hinge is much less stressed.

The second method is to set your terrarium 1 to 2 inches (2.5–5.1 cm) off the flat surface on blocks or legs. A tightly fitting framed front can then be merely slipped over the open side (if this is divided in half, it will be easier to restrain nervous specimens).

Desert Terrarium

Many terrestrial and rock-dwelling (saxicolous) gecko species are desert dwellers. These, of course, survive best if provided with a terrarium simulating a desert habitat. Like the basic cage, this can be as large or as small, as complex or as simple, as prudence dictates. The sizes and activity patterns of your specimens should always be carefully considered.

The substrate: Although many herpetoculturists caution against the use of sand as a substrate (citing intestinal impactions if it is ingested by the gecko inhabitants), I have always used it successfully. In more than 40 years of gecko keeping, I have never lost a single specimen to impaction and, after all, what is a desert if not sand? I would recommend smooth-desert sand rather than sharp-sided silica play sand or aquarium gravel. However, if the chance of sand-related problems does worry you, the use of smooth, variably sized rocks can also be considered.

The depth of the substrate can vary. If only a fine covering is used, your tank will, of course, be lighter and easier to move and handle. If a thick layer of substrate is used, you will be able to better maintain the barely dampened bottom

When provided with a substrate, this simple cage can house a pair of small terrestrial geckos. A Central American banded gecko is shown.

layer and the dry top layer preferred by some gecko species. Rock ledges and caves, individual basking rocks, potted arid-land plants, cork bark hiding areas, and cholla cactus skeletons can be provided both for decoration and the psychological well-being of your specimen(s).

Because most desert-dwelling reptiles are adapted to low humidity, the top of your desert terrarium should be screen. This will prevent a buildup of internal humidity that could be detrimental to the health of your lizard.

Savanna Terrarium

Savannas are areas of transition between or at the edge of forest, woodland, or desert. Spacious, rolling glades, these (often) sparsely vegetated areas are the habitats of many gecko species. Different soil formation and moderate rainfall provide a habitat much different from that of either surrounding desert or woodland and forest.

Savannas often host various species of moderately, or at least seasonally, lush grasses, as well as thornscrub and other formidably armed trees. Areas of rocky scree may be present.

clumped grasses, as well as weathered branches, cactus skeletons, and strategically placed rocks and rock formations can be used for decorative purposes. The savanna terrarium plant community will require somewhat more water than that of the desert terrarium. However, even with judicious care, many (especially the grasses) will need replacing each season. The plants can be either potted or planted directly into the terrarium substrate. I prefer the latter, for many gecko species enjoy digging their burrows into and beneath the plant's root systems. A screen top will assist you in keeping the low humidity preferred by most savanna-dwelling gecko species.

Woodland and Forest Terrariums

Woodland and forest terrariums can be utilized for those geckos of humid, rainy temperate and tropical origins.

Plants: Because of the host of easily grown potted house plants and scientifically formulated soils that are available, woodland and forest terrariums are among the most easily constructed and maintained of the various terrarium types. Besides, the plants, attractive branches, and rocks work well as decorative and functional objects in the woodland and forest terrariums.

To successfully maintain your plants, it will be necessary to assure that their roots remain damp (but not soggy) and to provide them with adequate lighting. Even shade-tolerant philodendrons, pothos, and syngoniums will require several hours of fairly strong light daily if they are to survive.

The substrate: When constructing a woodland terrarium, I suggest first placing 1 to 2 inches (2.5–5.1 cm) of pea-size gravel as the base of the substrate. Atop this I lay a thickness or two of air-conditioning filter material cut to the exact size of the terrarium.

T I P

Avoiding Electrical Accidents

It is important to use caution when handling electrical equipment and wiring, which are particularly hazardous when used in connection with water. Always observe the following safeguards carefully:

✔ Before using any of the electrical equipment described in this book, check to be sure that it carries the UL symbol.
✔ Keep all lamps away from water or spray.
✔ Before using any equipment in water, check the label to make sure it is suitable for underwater use.
✔ Disconnect the main electrical plug before you begin any work in a terrarium containing water or touch any equipment.
✔ Be sure that the electric current you use passes through a central fuse box or circuit-breaker system. Such a system should be installed only by a licensed electrician. UV incandescent, full-spectrum fluorescent, and heat lamps are available at most pet and hardware stores.

Savannas are often subjected to weather extremes in the form of temperature, rainfall, or other such climatic vagaries. The plant community found in savannas is difficult to maintain in terrariums over extended periods. Periodic refurbishing of your terrarium vegetation will most likely be necessary.

The substrate: A thick layer of sandy humus into which a liberal helping of variably sized rocks has been mixed should comprise the substrate of the savanna terrarium. Seedling acacias and

The overall color and pattern of the spear-point leaf-tailed gecko blends remarkably well with the leaves of its forest home.

This latter prevents the 2 to 3 inches (5.1–7.6 cm) of soil that comes next from filling the spaces between the gravel. The rocks below the air-conditioning filters act as a reservoir that will prevent excess water from destroying the roots of your plants if you should happen to overwater.

Of course, if you regularly overwater, the reservoir will become filled and provide little benefit to the setup.

A glass or plastic top will help retain the high humidity preferred by many of the denizens of these habitats. If the humidity remains too high, it can be reduced by substituting a screen, or a combination screen and glass cover, for the full glass one.

Watering Techniques

Water Dishes

Some arboreal geckos will lap water from dishes in elevated positions. This is especially so if the surface of the water is roiled by a bubbling aquarium air stone.

Many but not all terrestrial geckos will lap water from dishes. If your specimens are reluctant to drink still water, the technique of roiling the water surface with a bubbling aquarium air stone will usually solve the problem.

Misting

Not all geckos will use water dishes. This is especially true of persistently arboreal species, which in nature lap dew and raindrops from leaves and limbs. Gently misting your terrarium

(until pendulous droplets form on leaves and perches) is the most suitable way of providing water for your arboreal geckos. Do this daily.

Hydration Chamber

The uses and benefits of hydration chambers have long been appreciated by zoos and other public institutions. They are only now coming into general use by private herpetoculturists and hobbyists.

The term "hydration chamber" is merely an overstated way of saying rain chamber. But there is nothing overstated about the rain chamber's value to the herpetoculturist. These receptacles can make the difference between life and death for dehydrated lizards (or any other reptiles or amphibians).

The use of a hydration chamber can do much to help moisture-starved reptiles recuperate. Those that will most benefit from such a structure are the rain forest species that are shipped long distances to reach the pet markets of America, Asia, Europe, and other countries.

Among others, the various Madagascar leaf-tailed geckos and rain forest species of bent-toed geckos are prime candidates for hydration chamber treatment. Desert species will rarely, if ever, need this sort of treatment.

Making your own: A hydration chamber can be constructed of wire mesh over a wood frame, or of an aquarium equipped with a circulating water pump and a screen or perforated Plexiglas top.

If you are fortunate enough to live in a benign climate where the cage can be placed outdoors, a mist nozzle can be placed on the end of a hose and affixed over the cage. Fresh water may be run through this for an hour or more a day. (If your community chlorinates or adds chloramines to the water supply, the "mist nozzle" technique can be detrimental to amphibians, all of which have permeable skins.

Treated water is less problematic for reptiles.)

If indoors, the cage can be placed on top or inside of a properly drained utility tub and the fresh water system used. It is imperative that the drain system be adequate and kept free of debris if this system is used indoors. A secondary (back-up) drain (just in case) might do much to guarantee your peace of mind.

In contained systems, the circulation pump forces water from the tank itself through a small diameter PVC pipe into which a series of lateral holes has been drilled, or merely brought up to the top of the tank and allowed to drip through the screen or perforated Plexiglas.

It is imperative that the water in self-contained systems be kept immaculately clean.

Cage Furnishings

Cage furnishings for geckos can be either primarily functional or, more usually, both functional and decorative.

Among the primarily functional examples are such items as hot rocks and heating limbs. Rock formations and caves that provide both beauty and a hiding area for your geckos, or sturdy-leafed plants and limbs that provide both perches and visual barriers as well as adding beauty to the terrarium, are perfect examples of the dual purpose cage furnishings.

Rocks

If multilayered rock formations or caves are provided, the rocks should be held in place (and together) with a nontoxic adhesive. Silicone

*The chocolate house gecko, **Hemidactylus fasciatus**, is one of the prettier species of the genus.*

aquarium sealant is quite satisfactory for this purpose. If even a single flat rock is placed on the surface of the sand, make absolutely certain that it cannot shift and injure your gecko should your pet burrow beneath it. Natural rocks provide better clawholds for your specimens than do the decorative glass rocks.

Wood and Cork

Bleached manzanita and other gnarled woods are often available at pet shops or from the wild. These provide perches and visual barriers for terrarium inhabitants. Cork bark comes in many shapes and sizes. It is available in small tubes into which shy geckos can retire if they choose, or in curved lengths, which can provide lightweight caves when laid atop the terrarium's substrate.

Plants

Plants of many types are readily available and serve many purposes when placed in a terrarium. As mentioned earlier, stiff-leafed types such as sansevierias or aloes can serve as both perches and visual barriers. Additionally, some gecko species like to place their eggs in the basal rosette of sansieveria leaves. If misted, the leaves of these (or any other) plants can provide drinking stations for your geckos.

Terrarium Cleanliness

Terrarium cleanliness is one of the most important aspects of successful gecko husbandry. The substrate should be changed or washed frequently, the perches should be scraped and washed as necessary, and all hard surfaces, such as rocks and glass, should be periodically cleaned and sterilized. Water, whether in bowls or daily mists, must be fresh and clean.

Fortunately, geckos are relatively small lizards that are not sloppy feeders. Keeping a gecko cage clean is usually rather easy. Terrestrial geckos usually choose a corner of their tank in which to defecate, so this area will need to be changed more frequently than the rest of the substrate. Similarly, arboreal geckos may choose a particular perch or a corner as their stooling area. Again, these areas will need frequent cleaning.

If you are using a sand substrate, it can be washed, sterilized, dried, and reused. Dirty wood chips or mulch should be discarded and new ones used. To sterilize sand, perches, twigs, rocks, cork bark, cholla skeletons, and the terrarium itself, a diluted solution of either Ro-Cal or chlorine bleach should be used. After cleaning and sterilizing the items, be sure all are thoroughly rinsed with clean, fresh water.

Terrarium cleanliness will do much to assure the long-term good health of your geckos. Regular cleaning will help prevent the spread of both diseases and endoparasites. The cleaning of terrariums should be a prominent part of your husbandry regimen.

The Texas banded gecko, Coleonyx brevis, is the smallest member of the genus.

Heating Your Terrarium

The way you should provide heat to your geckos will depend on the habits of the species of gecko involved. Fortunately, many heat sources are available today that were not even thought about a decade ago. Among these are hot rocks, heating branches, under-tank heaters, sub-sand heating pads, heat tapes, ceramic heating units that screw into regular bulb fixtures, and, of course, heat bulbs.

Many of these implements are thermostatically controlled, others are of low wattage, hence low heat, but some may require that a rheostat or thermometer be incorporated into the circuitry by the purchaser.

Here are some facts that should be considered.

When it comes to thermoregulation, geckos embrace three lifestyles:
✔ Heliothermic (sun-basking, day-active species).
✔ Thigmothermic species (those that thermoregulate by lying on or against a previously warmed object such as a rock, tree limb, or even a road surface). Most nocturnal geckos are thigmotherms.
✔ Those that live in geographic areas having temperatures so ideal that little additional warming is necessary.

Heat Lamp

For heliotherms a heat lamp is ideal. Basking surface temperatures of between 88 and 94°F (31.1–34.4°C) are suitable. It would seem that overhead lighting is as necessary for the psychological well-being of these species as for the warmth provided. If the animals are agonistic (antagonistic toward each other), more than a single basking area may need to be provided. In any event, be sure to provide a thermal gradient (warm to cool). Cooler areas to which the specimen(s) can retire if necessary are mandatory.

Other Heat Sources

Many sources of supplementary heat are available for thigmotherms. Among these are the various hot rocks, heat limbs, under-tank heaters, and heat tapes. Of all, the under-tank heaters seem most reliable. Hot rocks have not only been known to malfunction (overheating and burning the specimens that use them); they can be difficult to keep clean of feces and uric acid, as well.

The newly available heat limbs or branches seem ideal for many nocturnal arboreal geckos.

Many under-tank heaters are thermostatically controlled. Some herpetoculturists build a back-up thermostat into the unit as a safeguard. Only a part (one-half or slightly less) of the tank should be heated. This will allow a thermal gradient

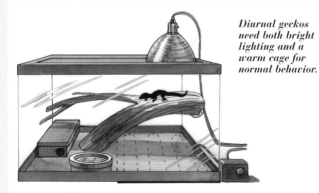

Diurnal geckos need both bright lighting and a warm cage for normal behavior.

HEATING

within the terrarium that your gecko will appreciate and use to advantage.

Lighting Your Terrarium

Is full-spectrum lighting necessary for your gecko? The role of full-spectrum lighting in gecko husbandry is poorly understood. It would seem that full-spectrum lighting is less necessary to the well-being of nocturnal forms than it is for diurnal geckos. It has been conclusively shown that light rays in the ultraviolet (UV) spectrum are beneficial to all basking reptiles.

The emissions in the UV-A band promote natural behavior in reptiles, whereas those in the UV-B length have been shown to enhance the synthesis of vitamin D_3. Vitamin D_3, in turn, enhances the absorption of calcium. Without full-spectrum lighting, dietary augmentation with D_3 and calcium is necessary on a frequent basis (these should be provided in greatest quantity to gravid females and rapidly growing juveniles). With full-spectrum lighting the dietary augmentations can be less frequent.

Without vitamin D_3, calcium is only poorly metabolized by reptiles.

Natural unfiltered sunlight remains the best full-spectrum lighting available. Where temperatures are warm (southern Florida and the lower Rio Grande Valley of Texas) it is possible to leave cages outdoors year-round. Wood and wire cages allow the diurnal geckos to bask at will in unfiltered sunshine.

On cool winter days, even some of the nocturnal species may bask, although they are probably partaking of the warmth provided rather than the sunlight itself.

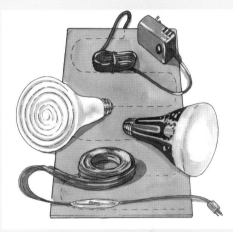

There are lighting and heating sources for every gecko habitat.

In passing through most types of glass and Plexiglas, the beneficial rays normally provided by sunlight are filtered out. However, the glass of the terrarium will concentrate the heat and quickly kill even the most heat-tolerant of reptiles. Care should be taken that glass terrariums are never placed outdoors in the full sunlight. Satisfactory artificial full-spectrum lighting is now available in both fluorescent and incandescent formats.

Although plant-grow bulbs are not full-spectrum, they are ideal for enhancing the growth of live plants in the terrarium. Additionally, if their warmth is directed to a basking perch or other such area, these bulbs can provide a suitable hot spot in which diurnal geckos may bask. Warmed basking areas can be provided equally well by regular incandescent flood bulbs, but these are not as effective for inducing plant growth.

YOUR GECKO'S HEALTH

When you are ready to purchase a gecko, start by determining the species you want and then find a reliable and knowledgeable seller. If you are purchasing from an Internet source, ask for references. It is very important that you choose a healthy gecko.

Choosing a Healthy Gecko

Ascertaining good health may not be quite as easily accomplished with geckos as with some other lizards but there are a few cues that signal caution when choosing one for a pet.

Eyes: The eyes of an alert, healthy gecko are not sunken or dull.

Coloration: Color can be a cue to health, but don't act in haste. A frightened gecko will often assume the darker hues usually associated with poor health. If left undisturbed for a few minutes, the lizard's normal brilliance should return.

Weight: Look at the overall size and body weight of the gecko. Although some gecko species are normally very slender, neither pelvis nor ribs should be prominently apparent.

A protruding pelvis or accordion ribs indicate an unnatural thinness that may be associated

Phelsuma madagascariensis kochi, Koch's day gecko, is another large subspecies of the giant day gecko coveted by hobbyists.

with improper diet, dehydration, parasitism, or other problems. Reversing this problem may not be possible for, like most reptiles, geckos are slow to show illness until it is far advanced.

Until you become familiar with the creatures, when choosing a gecko it is always best if you take a knowledgeable person—one who knows geckos—with you. Many species are normally hardy, some are normally delicate, but you will have a better chance with all if you start off with a healthy example.

Skin Shedding

The growth rate and overall health of your specimen will have much to do with the frequency with which it sheds its skin. The process results from thyroid activity. A day or two prior to shedding, the colors of your gecko will appear to fade. As the old keratinous layer loosens from the new one forming beneath it, your gecko may take on an overall grayish or

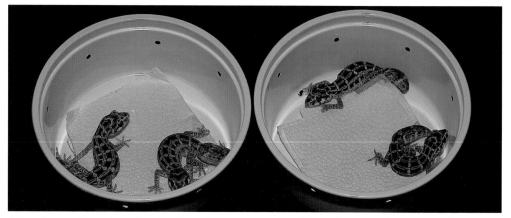

When being shipped, geckos (such as these viper geckos, Teratolepis fasciatus*) are placed in deli cups, then in insulated cartons.*

silvery sheen. When shedding has been completed, your specimen will again be as brightly marked as it was to begin with.

Problems in Shedding

Although it seems that wild geckos seldom have problems shedding, some captives may. Shedding problems may often be associated with

---

TIP

Handle with Care

Be careful when you handle a gecko. Remember, the skin of many geckos will tear readily if the lizards are grasped. This is especially true of the phelsumas. You simply cannot handle these little lizards safely. Having the fragile integument tear under your grasp is very disconcerting for you and more traumatic for the lizard.

---

newly imported lizards, those that are dehydrated or in otherwise suboptimal condition, or when the relative humidity in the gecko terrarium/cage is too low. Shedding problems are most often associated with toes and tail tips where the skin must be very carefully manually removed by the keeper. If not removed, the old dry skin may result in toe or tail tip loss. If patches of skin adhere, a gentle misting with tepid water may help your gecko rid itself of the pieces.

Safe Handling

Do's and don'ts: Most geckos should be considered display animals only. That is, they should be watched and appreciated but not handled. This is especially true of those whose skin tears easily (*Phelsuma, Ailuronyx, Teratoscincus*) or those that autotomize their tail easily (*Teratoscincus*). It is best to shepherd most species into a cardboard tube, jar, glass, or other such receptacle rather than to manually grasp them. Indeed, the skin of *Ailuronyx seychellensis* is so easily torn that it has been given the common name of "skin-sloughing gecko."

Some geckos (*Gekko gecko* and *Gekko smithi*, among others) can and will bite a hand painfully hard if carelessly restrained.

Caution: Even such relatively easy-to-handle specimens as leopard and fat-tailed geckos do not like to be grasped. However, these species will often crawl rather confidently into your hand where they can then be gently cupped with the other hand. It is important that terrestrial geckos not be allowed to crawl out of your hand and drop to the ground. Such a drop can result in internal damage, broken limbs, and/or autotomized tail. Although arboreal species that are more adapted to jumping, dropping, or actually falling may suffer less from accidental falls, they still should not be handled carelessly.

Gecko Fears

Geckos are alert lizards that usually perceive an approaching hand as having predatory intentions and will dart away quickly as the hand nears. You should honor the reluctance of these lizards to be handled. Handling your geckos

CHECKLIST

Choosing a Gecko

✔ When choosing a gecko, select one with typical color, good (normal) body weight. Make sure the eyes are not sunken or dull.
✔ Choose one that moves quickly and alertly when it is disturbed.
✔ If in a communal terrarium and all but one gecko dart quickly away when disturbed, do not choose the one that remains quiescent. This is more apt to be a sign of ill health than of tolerance.
✔ If given good care, geckos are wonderful and usually long-lived lizards. If you choose yours carefully, chances are that you will become a satisfied hobbyist.

little and providing them with surroundings in which they feel secure will promote good health and perhaps even be an important prelude to successful breeding programs.

The shedding skin is easily seen on this gold-dust day gecko and is often eaten by the lizard as it is discarded.

The yellow-backed gecko, Gekko ulikovskii, is smooth-skinned and slender.

As shown here, ventilation holes (or a screen top) are usually needed. This is a Mocquard's ocelot gecko, Paroedura bastardi.

Quarantine

To prevent the spread of diseases and parasites between geckos, it is important that you quarantine new specimens for at least a week (a month is better). This means that the lizard should be in a cage by itself, and that you make sure you do not transmit any possible pathogens by washing your hands before and after you clean its cage, change its water, or examine the lizard itself. During quarantine, take the time just to watch your lizard. During this time, fecal exams should be carried out to determine whether or not endoparasites are present. For this, you simply take a stool specimen to your reptile veterinarian.

The quarantine area should be completely removed from the area in which other reptiles are kept—preferably in another room.

The quarantine tank should be thoroughly cleaned prior to the introduction of the new lizard(s) and it should be regularly cleaned throughout the quarantine period. As with any

This Tibetan frog-eyed gecko, Teratoscincus roborowskii, *is alert and will probably bite a finger if prodded.*

other terrarium, the quarantine tank should be geared to the needs of the specimen that it is to house. Temperature, humidity, size, lighting, and all other factors must be considered.

Only after you (and your veterinarian) are completely satisfied that your new specimen(s) are healthy and habituated should they be brought near other specimens.

Parasites

Whether captive-bred or wild-collected, many geckos harbor internal parasites. Because of the complexities of identification of endoparasites and the necessity to accurately weigh

specimens before treatment and dosages can be determined, the eradication of internal parasites is best left to a qualified reptile veterinarian.

Because geckos are such small creatures there is no room for error when calculating medications.

DIETS

Most geckos are nocturnal and insectivorous, ghosting over trees, rocks, or dwellings in pursuit of their insect prey on warm, still nights. A few geckos are omnivorous, consuming fruit, nectar, pollen, flower parts, and sweet saps besides the more usual insect prey.

Getting Started

Although most geckos are basically insectivorous, some larger species will also prey on the nestlings of mice and small birds. Additionally, many lap a fair amount of pollen, nectar, sweet tree saps, and exudate from soft, overripe fruit. Learn the diet of your gecko before acquisition.

Healthy geckos usually feed readily; those in poor health may be difficult to induce to feed. If your gecko does not feed readily, make sure that terrarium conditions are optimum and that the lizard is well hydrated.

Insects

A poorly fed or otherwise unhealthy insect offers little but bulk when fed to your gecko. To have a healthy lizard, the feed insects must themselves be healthy. Feed and house all feed insects well before you offer them to your

An occasional pinky mouse is relished by many leopard (and other large terrestrial) geckos.

geckos. If the insects are not healthy, your geckos may be slowly starving.

Gut-loading is a term you should get to know well. Gut-loading simply means that before offering them to your gecko(s) the feed insects are fed an abundance of highly nutritious foods.

Calcium, vitamin D_3, fresh fruit and vegetables, fresh alfalfa and/or bean sprouts, honey and vitamin-mineral enhanced (chick) laying mash, and commercial cricket food are only a few of the foods that may be considered for gut-loading insects.

Insects quickly lose much of their food value if not continually fed an abundance of highly nourishing foodstuffs. Except for field plankton, grasshoppers, and locusts, all feed insects (including silkworms and houseflies) are now commercially available. Most (especially crickets, waxworms, and mealworms) will be available at neighborhood pet stores. Sources for all, including those mentioned, can be found on the Internet or in the classified sections of reptile magazines.

Crickets

The gray cricket (*Acheta domesticus*) is now bred commercially by the millions both for fishing bait and for pet food.

Other species may be collected from beneath debris in fields, meadows, and open woodlands. If available in suitable sizes, all species of crickets are ideal for gecko food. Feed the crickets fresh calcium-D_3-dusted carrots, potatoes, broccoli, oranges, squash, sprouts, chick-laying mash, or a commercial cricket diet. Provide the insects water by placing cotton balls, a sponge, or even pebbles or aquarium gravel in a shallow dish of water.

House crickets in an aquarium or smooth-sided trash can. Provide the insects crumpled newspapers, the center tubes from rolls of paper towels, or other such materials. Paper towel tubes can be lifted and the requisite number of crickets shaken from inside them into the lizard's cage or a transportation jar. This makes handling the fast-moving, agile insects easy.

Grasshoppers and Locusts

Grasshoppers and locusts (*Shistocerca* sp. and *Locusta* sp. in part) are widely used as reptile foods in European and Asian countries but are seldom commercially available in the United States. They can be field-collected by deftly wielding a field net. However, grasshoppers are fast, and it may take some time for you to build up your netting skills. You may wish to remove the large hopping legs before you place these insects in with your geckos.

Waxworms

The waxworm (*Galleria* sp.) is really a caterpillar, the larval stage of the wax moth that frequently infests neglected beehives. They have a very high fat content and should be fed to geckos only on occasion. Waxworms are available commercially from many sources. They are

frequently used as fish bait and are available from bait stores.

Feed them chick-laying mash, wheat germ, honey, and yeast mixed into a syrupy paste.

Giant Mealworms

Giant mealworms (*Zoophobas* sp.) are the larvae of a South American wood-boring beetle. They can be fed a diet of chicken starting mash, bran, leafy vegetables, and apples. These are readily available from all traditional sources.

Mealworms

Long a favorite of neophyte reptile and amphibian keepers, mealworms (*Tenebrio molitor*) contain a great deal of chitin and should actually be fed sparingly. They are easily kept and bred in plastic receptacles containing a 2- to 3-inch (5.1–7.6-cm) layer of bran (available at your local livestock feed store) for food and a potato or apple for their moisture requirements. It takes no special measures to breed these insects.

Roaches

Although roaches can be bred, it is nearly as easy to collect these as needed. Roaches, of one or more species, are present in much of the world. The size of the roach proffered must be tailored to the size of the geckos being fed. A meal of several small roaches is usually better than a meal consisting of one or two large ones.

Termites

Collect fresh termites as necessary. They are usually easily found during rainy or humid weather beneath the bark in dead pine trees. Should you decide to hold onto extras, they may be kept in some of the slightly dampened wood in which you originally found them.

Fruit–Honey Diet

Formulas for making the fruit-honey preferred by day geckos, leafy-tailed geckos, and giant geckos are contained in the section on day geckos (page 85). This liquefied, vitamin- and mineral-enhanced mixture is relished by many other species, as well.

An ornate day gecko licks a honey-fruit mixture from a small cup.

BREEDING BASICS

Although many geckos breed well in captivity with little concerted preparation, other species do so only sparingly and then require rather extensive conditioning. Conditioning, as used here, relates to A-1 health, suitable body weight, and reproductive cycling.

Cycling

Cycling refers to a physiological readying of your gecko for breeding. Under natural conditions, the life cycles of geckos are influenced by seasonal climatic changes. Influencing factors include temperature, rainfall, relative humidity, and photoperiod. The lives of specific gecko species may be affected by some or all of these factors. For instance, seasonal changes in temperature and photoperiod, which are less at the equator than in temperate areas, would influence the activity and lifestyle of equatorial geckos less than it would those of species from temperate areas. Changes in relative humidity and rainfall would figure prominently in the habits of tropical species.

To a lesser degree, these annual seasonal changes can (and if you hope to breed some of

Displaying a trait common to many geckos, this female neon day gecko is drying and placing her eggs in a site she has carefully chosen.

the more demanding gecko species, must) be duplicated in the terrarium.

Photoperiod: Photoperiod can be easily duplicated by using a reversed electric eye to turn terrarium lights on and off at dawn and dusk. This can also be done manually, or with a simple timer, changing the time settings a little each week (check the weather page in your local newspaper for sunrise and sunset times, and note how these times change as the seasons progress). It may take specimens imported from southern latitudes a season or two to acclimate to the reversed seasons of northern latitude herpetoculturists.

Temperature: Temperature, both daily and seasonal, can be altered with the prudent use of lights and/or heating elements. Temperatures should be allowed to drop slightly on summer nights and slightly more during the shortest days of the year. Some geckos may actually require a month or so of semi-brumation (the reptilian equivalent of hibernation) during the winter months to attain reproductive readiness.

The termite-eating, burrowing South African barking gecko, Ptenopus garrulous, *has a loud, easily heard call.*

Humidity: Rainfall can be simulated and seasonally altered by expedient misting techniques. Relative humidity within the cage can be altered by partially or completely covering the terrarium with glass, Plexiglas, or sheet plastic, or by covering or removing plastic covering from outdoor or wire and wood-frame cages.

Feeding

Your geckos should be fed most heavily during the long, warm, humid days of summer. As you allow the temperatures to cool, reduce the amounts you feed. With warming temperatures, you should again increase the amount of food fed to the geckos. Offer pinkie mice to geckos large enough to eat them. Gut-loaded crickets, roaches, and mealworms are also ideal.

Be sure to provide plenty of calcium and vitamin D_3 throughout the year. These additives are especially important at the time of eggshell formation by adult female geckos and for proper bone development and the growth of hatchlings and juveniles.

Species such as leopard geckos and many of the day geckos are easily bred. Others such as African fat-tails and the various bent-toed species are more difficult. To succeed with many, you may need to experiment with the various cycling factors. With time, as your experiences broaden, you will find yourself making informed decisions and extrapolating from earlier successes. With these experiments will come more successes. Record and share methods, successes, and even failures. All will combine to help you and others with future herpetocultural projects.

TIP

Seasonal Conditions

For the most part you should strive to have the lowest humidity, the fewest hours of daylight, and the lowest temperatures in midwinter. The greatest amount of all three would be provided in midsummer.

Reproduction

In most cases, it is incubation temperatures, rather than genetics, that determine the sex of geckos. This is referred to as temperature-dependent sex determination (TDSD). Cool temperatures produce female geckos; overly warm ones will produce males. Eggs incubated at neutral temperatures produce both male and female hatchlings.

Parthenogenesis

Some gecko species, such as the Indo-Pacific gecko, *Hemidactylus garnotii*, and the mourning gecko, *Lepidodactylus lugubris*, are all females and reproduce parthenogenetically. Parthenogenesis may yet be found to occur in other gecko species.

Parthenogenetic females produce viable eggs without male fertilization. The young geckos so produced are always females.

Although popular hypothesis claims parthenogenesis to be an efficient mode of reproduction, this may not be true. Current scholarly trends of thought are that vertebrate parthenogenesis is not as effective a means of reproduction in the long run as heterosexuality. Additional long-term studies are needed.

Pseudocourtship

A stylized courtship (called pseudocourtship) stimulates ovulation. In Florida and Hawaii *H. garnotii* lay eggs throughout the warmer months of the year.

Reproduction: The vast majority of geckos are oviparous (egg-laying). Depending on the species, the eggs may have hard, calcareous shells or pliable (and permeable) parchmentlike ones.

A very few gecko species are ovoviviparous, producing two living young per clutch.

Many male geckos bear a small protuberance (anal spur) on each side of the hemipenial bulge.

Ovoviviparity: Live-bearing in the geckos is restricted to one subfamily, found in the Southern Hemisphere. Geckos of the subfamily Diplodactylinae that bear living young include:
• All members of the New Zealand genus *Heteropholis*.
• All members of the New Zealand genus *Hoplodactylus*.
• Both species of the New Zealand genus *Naultinus*.
• *Rhacodactylus trachyrhynchos*, New Caledonia.

Oviparous Geckos

Hard-shelled eggs: Two subfamilies in the family Gekkonidae produce hard-shelled eggs. These are Gekkoninae, the typical geckos (usually there are two eggs per clutch) and the Sphaerodactylinae, the reef gecko and allies (usually just one egg per clutch).

above: Note the pattern variations in these hatchling Central American banded geckos.

right: A hatchling Henkel's leaf-tailed gecko, Uroplatus henkeli, has just emerged from one of the eggs.

A leopard gecko emerges from its egg.

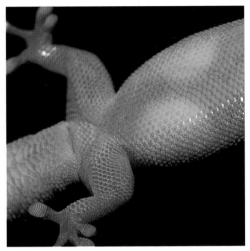

As shown in this photo of a female neon day gecko, developing eggs may be seen through the ventral skin of many species.

Soft-shelled eggs: Most species in the subfamily Diplodactylinae, of the Gekkonidae, lay soft-shelled eggs, as do all members of the family Eublepharidae, the eyelid geckos. Both of these groups usually have two eggs per clutch.

Choosing the Deposition Site

Three types of deposition sites are usually chosen by gravid female geckos. There are also three kinds of eggs.

The three deposition sites are
✔ arboreal
✔ rock-face
✔ terrestrial.

The three kinds of eggs are
✔ hard-shelled adhesive
✔ hard-shelled nonadhesive
✔ soft-shelled nonadhesive.

TIP

Breeding Precautions

Geckos that are underweight or in poor health should not be bred. Egg production and deposition can be very taxing. It can be as difficult to successfully breed obese specimens as underweight ones, although the process is less taxing for overweight geckos than for thin ones.

Arboreal: Arboreal sites can be used by both egg-gluing and non-egg-gluing gecko species. Captive egg-gluers may place their eggs on terrarium glass or the leaves of stiff-leafed plants; nongluers will often use the central rosettes of plants such as sansevierias or bromeliads for deposition sites.

Rock faces: Rock faces (including crevices and exfoliations) can be used by either egg-gluing or non-egg-gluing species.

Terrestrial: Both hard-shelled and soft-shelled-producing gecko species may construct a deposition site in the substrate. They dig directly into the substrate, often burrowing under a rock.

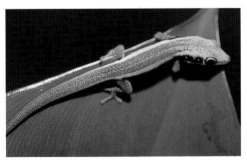

A hatchling neon day gecko.

HOW-TO: INCUBATION

Although it is possible to hatch gecko eggs without using an incubator, maintaining the correct temperature parameters can then be a haphazard and difficult task. Incubators of many makes and models, from inexpensive to almost unaffordable, are readily available.

A boon to the successful hatching of gecko eggs was made available by Hovabator when it introduced an affordable line of reptile egg incubators. These are readily available from many sources and the lowest priced model costs about $55. Do not confuse this incubator with a chick-egg incubator for temperatures in

the latter are digitally preset and are too hot for reptile eggs.

Hovabator incubators will readily hold 50 to 100 gecko eggs and maintain temperatures well. Most models have a viewing port in the cover.

There are other makers of incubators as well, and the prices for some can be well over $500.

If it is possible to do so, move the gecko eggs to an incubator as soon as they are found. Keep the eggs oriented in the position they were found (do not turn them). If the eggs are produced by an egg-gluing species, they may be placed in irremovable situa-

tions (such as on terrarium glass). In this case it will be necessary to tape a small plastic cup containing a little moistened sphagnum over the eggs. It is best if the moss does not actually touch the eggs. It may be necessary to remoisten the moss periodically. Remember, you are striving for high humidity—not actual wetness.

Soft-shelled Eggs

The eggs of the eublepharine and diplodactyline geckos are soft-shelled and moisture-permeable. Therefore, incubation conditions need to be fairly precise. Both vermiculite and sphagnum make good incubation mediums. The vermiculite should be moistened with four parts of water to six parts of vermiculite, by weight. After it is thoroughly mixed, the eggs may be placed directly on the medium in a shallow depression. A shallow open dish of water in the incubator will help retain a high relative humidity. If sphagnum is used, it should be thoroughly moistened, then squeezed as dry as possible by hand. The eggs can be nestled directly amid the moss.

If the moss or vermiculite is too dry or too wet, the eggs

Tape the bottom half of a paper cup over eggs that are glued to the aquarium wall.

Incubation Guidelines

✔ Place eggs inside covered containers in the incubator. Use moistened vermiculite or sphagnum for the medium.

✔ Free-laid eggs can be placed atop a plastic lid and then carefully moved to the incubator.

✔ Keep the eggs oriented as they were when laid.

✔ Be sure to cover the egg containers when they are placed in the incubator.

✔ Soft-shelled eggs require a rather precise humidity and substrate moisture.

✔ Hard-shelled eggs of rain forest and other humidity-adapted geckos require a high relative humidity and do best if kept from direct contact with the substrate.

✔ The hard-shelled eggs of many desert and arid-land species develop best at a low relative humidity.

Free-laid eggs can be placed atop a plastic lid and then moved to the incubator.

Eggs are placed inside covered containers in the incubator. Use moistened vermiculite or sphagnum for the medium.

will desiccate or overhydrate, respectively. Both conditions can be fatal to the developing embryo.

Note: Incubation temperatures that are maintained between 84 and 87°F (28.9–30.6°C) will produce hatchlings of both sexes.

Hard-shelled Eggs

The incubation of the eggs of rain forest and other high-humidity gecko species seems most successful if the eggs do not actually touch the hatching medium (sit them atop a small plastic lid or other such support).

They will require a 90 to 100 percent relative humidity to develop properly. The hard-shelled eggs of many arid-land species will best develop at a 45 to 60 percent relative humidity. Hatching success also seems greater with these eggs when they are kept from directly touching the substrate.

Again, if the eggs are of an egg-gluing species it may be necessary to adopt special incubation techniques. Attempting to remove the eggs of an egg-gluing species from the area where the female placed them will usually result in damage to the eggs and death to the embryo.

TYPICAL GECKOS OF THE AMERICAS

Of the world's 700-plus species of geckos, only 27 occur in the United States and of these only five are natives. Geckos are limited in distribution to only the more southern states. Even in the comparatively benign climate of these latitudes, most gecko species seek protected areas, and populations of the eastern forms are often the densest amid clusters of buildings, such as dwellings and warehouses.

Two Families

The geckos of the continental United States represent two families, the Eublepharidae and the Gekkonidae. The former, pronounced "you-blef-fare-eh-dee," contains four species of western desert geckos. The eublepharines lack modified subdigital lamellae (toe pads) and have functional eyelids.

The remaining gecko species of the United States are all members of the family Gekkonidae (pronounced "geck-on-eh-dee") but represent two subfamilies. These are the typical geckos of the subfamily Gekkoninae (pronounced as above except for the last syllable, which is "nee"), and

Madagascar giant day geckos are now established in southern Florida.

the reef geckos and allies of the subfamily Sphaerodactylinae (pronounced "sfay-row-dack-til-lin-ae").

Typical Geckos

Eastern Geckos

Florida is the epicenter of gecko diversity in the eastern United States. With a single exception, this being the reef gecko, Florida's gecko fauna is considered to be of introduced status.

Some of Florida's geckos can be easily seen and found (various house and reef geckos), but others, such as the ocellated gecko, are seen so sporadically that between sightings speculation turns to the possibility of their having been eradicated.

Flat-tailed Gecko

The tiny flat-tailed gecko (*Cosymbotus platyurus*) currently occurs only in Pinellas and Lee counties, Florida. It was long a mainstay of the pet industry, being imported from Southeast Asia primarily as a food species for lizard-eating snakes. It is easily maintained and bred in captivity. It eats tiny insects and fruit-honey mixture.

Cosymbotus is noticeably flattened. Its broad tail has serrate edges, and there are skin flanges on the sides of its body and rear legs. When the lateral flanges are spread outward, this little

Bibron's gecko, **Pachydactylus bibroni,** *is robust and active.*

A yellow to orange belly typifies the Indo-Pacific gecko, **Hemidactylus garnotii,** *a now common house gecko in Florida.*

lizard casts little if any shadow. The toes are partially webbed and the toe pads are large. The pupils are vertical. This arboreal gecko is adult at about 3.5 inches (8.9 cm) in overall length. The flat-tailed gecko readily colonizes disturbed areas and human habitations. It is quite capable of changing its color, often being a unicolored, pasty cream at night and quite dark with numerous darker bands in the daytime.

Male flat-tailed geckos produce a series of clicks as advertisement calls or an easily heard, high-pitched squeak, if distressed.

Tokay Gecko

Not only is the tokay (*Gekko gecko*) the largest gecko in Florida (and one of the largest in the world), it is also the noisiest. Tokays have been found in several counties in Florida. Although often smaller, specimens nearing 1 foot (30.5 cm) in length may be encountered.

For years, tokays have been a mainstay of the pet industry. They remain so today. In the erroneous assumption that big geckos will rid their dwellings of roaches, people have released them in residences and office complexes throughout much of the United States. In southern Florida, where the benign, subtropical climate will allow the species to survive in the wild, tokays have expanded their ranges from the original points of release to neighboring structures. In urban areas, they may now be seen and heard in shade trees and palms, on power poles, and in other such habitats.

Tokays have loud voices. Their two-syllabled calls begin with a chuckle, evolve into a series

Tokay geckos, **Gekko gecko,** *are the most commonly seen species of the genus.*

of "geck-os" or "tokays," and end in lengthened, slurred notes.

These big geckos are primarily nocturnal, but may thermoregulate in sunny areas on mornings following cool nights.

Tokays are well able to overpower and consume other lizards, frogs, insects, and other arthropods, but may also accept nestling birds and rodents as well. If threatened with capture, tokays open their mouths widely, growl with a drawn out "gecccck," and, if hard-pressed, will jump toward the offending object and bite. They often retain their grip with a bulldog-like tenacity, tightening up at intervals to remind you that they're still there.

Although the consequences of a tokay bite are not serious (hardly more than any other prolonged pinch), it can be a frightening encounter for an unsuspecting person. These predaceous lizards are too well known by reptile enthusiasts to require much description. They are unmistakably colored, having orange and white markings against a gray or blue-gray ground color. The protuberant eyes may vary from yellow-green to orange. The pupils are complex and vertically elliptical. The toe pads are large and easily visible.

The hard-shelled, paired, adhesive-shelled eggs are deposited in secluded areas of buildings, tree hollows, or other like spots. With her hind feet, the female manipulates the eggs into the spot she has chosen. Wet and pliable when laid, the calcareous, moderately adhesive eggshell soon dries, holding the eggs in the

Mediterranean geckos, **Hemidactylus turcicus,** *have colonized many parts of the southern United States.*

desired spot. Each female may lay several clutches annually. The young exceed 3 inches (7.6 cm) at hatching. Communal nestings occur.

House Geckos

The geckos with which most Floridians are familiar are the various house geckos of the genus *Hemidactylus*. Called "house geckos" because of their fondness for buildings (including houses, warehouse complexes, hospitals, and schools), these little lizards become active at twilight and may gather around lit porch (or other) lights to prey on insects drawn to the glow.

There are now four species (two warty and two smooth scaled) of this genus established in Florida. Two of these, *H. turcicus*, the Mediterranean gecko, and *H. garnotii*, the Indo-Pacific gecko, have now expanded their ranges to other southern states as well. The various *Hemidactylus* species seem to be successively successful in their efforts at colonization, and where once the Mediterranean reigned supreme, it has now been replaced in many areas by the newer establishees. All of the "hemis" are quite capable of strong color changes. They are darker and (often) more heavily patterned by day, lighter and less contrastingly patterned by night.

The Big Bend gecko, Coleonyx reticulatus, *is found in western Texas and adjacent Mexico.*

✔ Pacific house gecko, *Hemidactylus frenatus*: This 5-inch (12.7-cm) long lizard is the most recently found member of this Floridian gekkonid quartet. It is mostly smooth-scaled and is typically quite light in color. It has a white to pale yellow belly. This species is known only from the Lower Keys and from Dade, Broward, and Lee counties on the mainland.
✔ The smooth-scaled Indo-Pacific gecko, *Hemidactylus garnotii*, an all-female, parthenogenic species, has some rather pronounced spinous scales on its tail. It has an orange belly. It may attain 5 inches (12.7 cm) in total length. Usually seen on buildings, it may often be seen on trees and amid debris of both natural and man-made origin. It is now found in many locations throughout Florida as well as Hawaii. Occasional examples have been found in Georgia and Alabama but it is not certain that they are established in these latter two states.
✔ The Mediterranean gecko, *H. turcicus*, is strongly tuberculate and obscurely patterned. The dorsal markings are never in the shape of a chevron. It has a spotty distribution from Florida to California and Hawaii and occurs also in many other southern states. It reaches a length of 5 inches (12.7 cm).
✔ The tropical house gecko, *Hemidactylus mabouia*, is the second of the warty house geckos in Florida. It is less strongly tuberculate than the Mediterranean gecko and a series of chevrons is present on the back. This gecko is often seen on tree trunks and debris piles well away from human habitation.

*Tarentola annularis, **the white-spotted gecko, has four white spots on its shoulders.***

The house geckos are most active on still, humid nights. They will be most easily found on the walls of dwellings and warehouse complexes. Be keenly observant as you approach the outer perimeters of the halos surrounding lit porch lights or other sources of outdoor illumination. House geckos are often vigilant and will be alerted to your presence from fair distances. If the geckos have been regularly persecuted by humans, they will be quick to seek cover. The males of all are capable of making weak squeaking sounds. They may vocalize during territorial scuffles or when captured by a human or other predator.

The Moorish Gecko and the White-spotted Gecko

Two wall geckos, the Moorish and the white-spotted (*Tarentola mauritanica* and *T. annularis*, respectively) are now present in the United States. The Moorish gecko has become established in south Florida and San Diego County, California. It is native to and most common along the warmer Mediterranean coastal areas but may be seen in some inland locations. It is also found on the Canary and Ionian Islands, Crete, and North Africa. The white-spotted gecko is a native of Africa, from Cameroon to Egypt. Both attain a heavy-bodied 6.5 inches (16.5 cm) in length.

The Moorish gecko has prominent tubercles arranged in well-separated rows along it's back, sides, and tail. All scales on regenerated tails are small. Prominent rounded tubercles are present on the sides of the neck. The coloration of this interesting lizard is of variable earthen tones that usually blend well with its background. The toe pads are prominent and extend to the very tips of the toes. The lamellae are single (undivided) across their entire width.

Although typically a dweller of rocky habitats, the Moorish gecko has become a house gecko in urbanized areas.

The white-spotted gecko has smoother skin and is typified by four white spots on the shoulders.

Both have clicking calls and are quite vocal. Because of their large size, the adults of these geckos can easily overpower and consume smaller geckos as well as insects.

Adult ashy geckos blend well with a leafy substrate.

Sphaerodactyline Geckos

Four species of these small geckos occur in the state of Florida. Three are in the genus *Sphaerodactylus* and one is in the genus *Gonatodes*. The three species of *Sphaerodactylus*, *S. notatus*, *S. elegans*, and *S. argus*, have rounded toe pads; *Gonatodes* lacks toe pads. All lack eyelids. Of the four, three are introduced. The reef gecko, *S. n. notatus*, is Florida's only native gecko species. All produce single eggs.

Ashy Gecko

The ashy gecko (*S. e. elegans*), a native of Cuba, is the most arboreal of this trio. It is also the largest (by nearly 0.5 inch [1.3 cm]) of the three Floridian species.

Considerable ontogenetic (age-related) color changes occur. Hatchlings are green with dark

crossbands and brilliant orange tails. Adults are dark with irregular light spots and dots and streaks. The color change from that of the juvenile to that of the adult is gradual. This species may be pasty white at night.

Ashy geckos climb well and can be abundant on trees, buildings, and other structures. They seem less common when house geckos are also present. They are both crepuscular and nocturnal. The ashy gecko is restricted in distribution to the Lower Keys.

Florida Reef Gecko

This gecko is abundant in leaf litter and debris in Dade and Monroe counties, Florida. It has also been found in coastal Broward and Palm Beach counties. Reef geckos are particularly abundant (or at least are most easily found) beneath tidal wrack. On some of Florida's Lower Keys it is not uncommon to find three or four of these minuscule lizards beneath boards and flotsam just above the high-tide line. Reef geckos are amazingly fast and adept at instantaneously disappearing into the tiniest of fissures or openings.

As it grows, the vivid hues of this hatchling ashy gecko, **Sphaerodactylus elegans,** *will dull to warm, ashy browns or grays.*

The four subspecies of banded geckos of the American West (this is the Tucson banded gecko, Coleonyx variegatus bogerti) are confusingly similar in appearance.

Principally terrestrial, both sexes of this dimorphic species are darker by day than night. The males are a study of dark on dark—deep brown specks against a slightly lighter ground color. Very old males may be nearly or entirely deep brown. Females are also dark-flecked, but have dark stripes on the head and usually a pair of light ocelli in a dark shoulder spot. The tails of both sexes may be just on the orange side of brown.

Ocellated Gecko and Yellow-headed Gecko

These are both very rare in Florida and seem restricted to Key West and Stock Island. The ocellated gecko, *sphaerodactylus a. argus*, has several pairs of light nape spots. Males of the yellow-headed gecko, *gonatodes albigularis fuscus,* bear a tan to yellow head and have a blackish green body. Except for a light collar, females are entirely mottled brown.

Eublepharine Geckos of the Americas

The New World eublepharine geckos are all in the genus *Coleonyx*. These geckos are best adapted to lives in sparsely vegetated, rocky arid

and semi-arid lands. Of the seven species, one, the western banded gecko (*Coleonyx variegatus*), is represented in our west by four subspecies. All eublepharines have functional eyelids, all lack toe pads, and all lay soft (parchmentlike) shelled eggs. All are of similar appearance, varying somewhat in size, markings (which can vary with age), and type of scalation.

Collectively, these are commonly known as the banded, reticulated, and barefoot geckos. Four species are common and regularly seen in the pet trade. These are the western banded gecko, *C. variegatus* ssp., the Texas banded gecko, *C. brevis*, the Mexican banded gecko, *C. elegans*, and the Central American banded gecko, *C. mitratus*. The remaining three species, the Big Bend gecko, *C. reticulatus*, the barefoot gecko, *C. switaki*, and the black-banded gecko, *C. fasciatus*, are protected and unavailable to hobbyists.

Western Banded Gecko and Texas Banded Gecko

In one or another of its seven subspecies (three in Mexico and four in the United States) the western banded gecko ranges from southwestern New Mexico to western central California and southward to the tip of the Baja

Peninsula and the northwestern Mexican mainland. None of the subspecies exceed 5.5 inches (13.9 cm) in length and they are usually smaller. Only those present in the United States are seen in the pet trade.

The Texas banded gecko is adult at a bit less than 5 inches (12.7 cm). This, the smallest of the species, ranges through western and southern Texas to southeastern New Mexico and northern Mexico.

Differentiating the Various United States Subspecies of the Many Banded Geckos

✔ The subspecies of *C. variegatus* have 6 to 10 preanal pores on each side that V smoothly at the midline. There are no tuberculate scales interspersed among the smooth dorsal or lateral scales.

• San Diego banded gecko, *C. v. abbotti*: dark bands have poorly defined or no light center and are of the same width or a bit narrower than the light bands; distinct light collar; southwestern California and most of the northern half of the Baja Peninsula.

• Tucson banded gecko, *C. v. bogerti*: dark bands with noticeably light centers about as wide as light interspaces or may be replaced by spots; eight or more preanal pores; southeastern Arizona, southwestern New Mexico, adjacent Mexico.

• Utah banded gecko, *C. v. utahensis*: dark bands wider than light interspaces and having very irregular edges; southwestern Nevada, adjacent southeastern Utah and northeastern Arizona.

• Desert banded gecko, *C. v. variegatus*: dark bands with noticeably light centers about as wide as light interspaces or may be replaced by spots; seven or fewer preanal pores; southern Nevada, western Arizona, southeastern California.

✔ *Coleonyx brevis* has six or fewer preanal pores on each side and the two rows are separated at the midline. There are no tuberculate scales interspersed among the smooth dorsal or lateral scales.

• Texas banded gecko, *C. brevis*: Dark bands are much broader than light interspaces and have irregular edges that may spike outward and connect with a dark spot in the light area.

✔ Big Bend gecko, *C. reticulatus*, is a large (to 7 inches [18 cm]) gecko that is banded when young and spotted when adult; it is liberally studded with tuberculate scales on the back and sides; a protected species, it occurs only in the Big Bend region of Texas and adjacent Mexico.

✔ Barefoot gecko, *C. switaki* is another large (to 6.5 inches [16.5 cm] long) gecko that is precisely marked with bands of light spots when young and is more obscurely patterned when adult; tuberculate scales are present on the back and sides. A protected species, it occurs only in the extreme southern California and on the Baja Peninsula.

✔ Black-banded gecko, *C. fasciatus*, a 5-inch-long (12.7-cm) dark-banded gecko of Sonora, Mexico, is protected and not available in the pet trade.

✔ Mexican banded gecko, *C. elegans*. Although usually banded (strongly so when young), some examples of this 5.5-inch-long (13.9-cm) gecko may have a broad, dark, middorsal stripe instead; the claws are hidden by a terminal scale, making this species appear clawless. This pretty gecko ranges southward from southern Mexico to Guatemala.

✔ Central American banded gecko, *C. mitratus* is similar in most respects to the Mexican banded gecko. This species has fully visible claws; it ranges from El Salvador and Nicaragua to Panama.

Banded geckos are most commonly seen shortly after dark when they emerge from daytime lairs to forage. At this time they may be seen crossing roadways, often with their tails raised over their backs. If startled they skitter away quickly, their tails writhing like that of an angry cat. The scales on the original tail of a banded gecko are arranged in whorls, and the tail is readily autotomized, either in part, or at the basal constriction.

Regeneration is rapid but, even when complete, apparent. The scalation and overall appearance of a regenerated tail is very different from that of the original.

Because of the high permeability of the shell, female eublepharine geckos must choose their egg deposition sites carefully. It is important that sufficient moisture is present in the substrate to prevent desiccation, but not so much that the embryos drown.

In captivity females will often choose a small container (plastic margarine containers are perfect) holding 1 to 2 inches (2.5–5.1 cm) of slightly moistened sand, vermiculite, or sphagnum moss.

Captive Care and Breeding

Many American geckos of both native and introduced species can be easily maintained and bred as captives. The methods of inducing breeding are pretty similar, no matter the species involved.

Housing

The terrarium: The size of the terrarium must vary according to the size and number of the species being held captive. For a pair or trio of small species such as the various house, reef, ashy, and yellow-headed, or banded geckos, a

TIP

Tokay Warning

Tokays are difficult to tame. They can and will bite hard if restrained. Although not serious, the bite can be painful, protracted, and disconcerting. Handle this gecko species with care!

10-gallon (37.9-L) terrarium is of adequate size. Because of the added height, a 15-gallon (56.8-L) show tank is better for the arboreal gecko species.

The substrate: One to 2 inches (2.5–5.1 cm) of fine sand is adequate as a substrate. Diagonal limbs are places upon which the geckos climb. This enables them to thermoregulate effectively, approaching the tanktop light more closely on cool days. The leaves on the bottom catch and retain droplets of water when the tank is misted, thus allowing a natural drinking method for the little lizards. A potted plant, such as a pothos or philodendron, placed in one corner of the tank will serve a like purpose for those geckos with more arboreal tendencies.

An in-tank temperature of between 74°F (23.3°C) and 88°F (31.1°C) should suffice. In warm climes, an incandescent tanktop reflector will retain such temperatures. In cooler climes, an under-tank heating pad may need to be used except during the summer months.

If you allow eggs deposited by your geckos to remain in the substrate, you must remember that a regimen of suitable relative humidity (85 to 100 percent) and incubation temperature (80 to 86°F [26.7–30°C]) must be retained if you expect the eggs to hatch. The humidity can be altered by judiciously misting the cage and substrate. The temperature can be regulated by attaching your heating unit to a thermostat. You may prefer to remove and incubate the eggs where humidity and temperature are more easily regulated. The same parameters as mentioned earlier should be maintained. Care must be used that the eggs are not turned (rotated) when they are moved. If this is done, the air sac is often disturbed and further development is arrested.

Nutrition

To retain the long-term health of your geckos, it is necessary that they be fed properly. Hatchlings will grow rapidly on a diet of termites, pinhead crickets, and aphids (in season). In Florida, the termites and aphids are easily found throughout much of the year. In more northerly areas, you may have to depend a little more heavily on the crickets and augment these with occasional treats of vestigial-winged fruit flies. These latter are initially available from biological supply houses and are easily raised once acquired.

Gut-loading the prey insects and dusting the baby crickets with a finely powdered supplement that contains both calcium and vitamin D_3 twice weekly will provide the vitamins and minerals needed for fast growing babies.

Although none of these gecko species are inveterate nectar feeders, they are occasionally given a bit of the vitamin-enhanced fruit concoction that is recommended for day geckos (see page 85 for recipe). Except for those that contain desert species, the gecko tanks are misted daily, care being taken that at least some of the surface leaves retain pendulous droplets for the geckos to drink.

Reproduction

Inducing breeding may involve nothing more complex than placing both sexes together, or it can be a little more complicated. Even in Florida, ovulation and spermatogenesis by geckos may be controlled by photoperiod (day length), relative humidity, and temperature. Thus, I have found almost all gecko species to breed seasonally, beginning with the lengthening days of spring and progressing into egg laying with the heightened relative humidity created by the advent of late spring and early summer rains. Mimicking these phenomena is rather easily done within the confines of a terrarium. By increasing the hours of illumination and misting the tank a little more frequently and making subtle temperature alterations, you may be able to induce breeding by your geckos at will.

Territoriality (male-to-male sparring and territory protection) is also important in inducing successful breeding. After successfully backing down a subordinate opponent, a dominant male gecko will often dash to a female, indulge in courtship, and breed her.

Sites: Although some of the little sphaerodactyline geckos might be termed egg-scatterers (merely laying their hard-shelled eggs amid the leaf litter of the woodland floor), others may place their eggs in tree-trunk hollows or in bark crevices, sometimes several feet above the ground. The rather thick-shelled eggs of the sphaerodactylines resist both desiccation and apparently, even if wet directly by rather sustained rains, overhydration.

Other female geckos, among them some of the house geckos, may also merely place their eggs among the leaves, but they seem to choose an area a little more carefully. Frequently their chosen deposition sites are also protected by additional debris or litter. Hollows beneath rocks, cinder blocks, logs, boards, newspapers, or discarded roofing shingles are seemingly favored. The eggs of some gecko species have adhesive shells and are placed high in hollow trees or near the eaves in buildings where they remain until hatching.

One such gecko is the tokay, Florida's largest alien species. Using her hind feet, she works the paired eggs into the area she has chosen. As she places the eggs, their shells are drying. By the time she has accomplished her task, the eggs have adhered and will remain so for the duration. So effective is the adhesion of the eggs that the hatched shells often remain in place for years, providing evidence of multiple clutching and even communal nesting practices.

Of the Florida geckos, only the tokay is too large to be kept in a 10- or 15-gallon (37.9–56.8-L) terrarium arrangement. For this large lizard a terrarium of from 29- to 50-gallon (109.8–189.3-L) size is suggested for a pair and a walk-in cage would be even better. In wire covered, wood-framed cages the females often choose the junction of an upright and the top to deposit their eggs, the incubation of which takes about 54 days.

In Florida's hot and humid atmosphere, no additional attention need be given the eggs. In an area with lower humidity, I would tape a cup containing a few spoonfuls of barely moistened sphagnum moss over the eggs (but not touching them). This would raise humidity and help retain an even temperature. In keeping with their large size, tokays also need larger food items than the other geckos of Florida. Mice, nestling birds, large roaches, adult crickets, grasshoppers, and other similar-sized prey items are all eagerly accepted.

Sex of Gecko as Determined by Temperature

Temperature (Fahrenheit)	Sex Produced
below 77°F	High egg mortality. Hatchlings will be females.
78 to 79°F	Females
80 to 83°F	Mostly females
84 to 86°F	Both sexes
87 to 89°F	Mostly males
90 to 91°F	Males
above 92°F	Heightened egg mortality. Hatchlings will be males.

As mentioned earlier, the various eublepharine geckos all lay eggs with thin, permeable shells. Gravid females will often enter a container holding a suitably moistened substrate (vermiculite, sphagnum moss, or even clean sand) to lay their eggs.

Egg deposition is usually accomplished at night. A proper substrate moisture content is critical to the development of the eggs. Although experience will ultimately prove the best teacher, mixing water and vermiculite (6 parts vermiculite to 4 parts water—by weight, not volume) will provide a suitably moist medium. The eggs are either laid on their side atop this or half buried in a shallow depression. Do not rotate the eggs when moving them. A shallow dish of water is often placed atop the vermiculite to assure a continuous high relative humidity.

The sex of many gecko species of both families is determined by temperature. Low temperatures produce females; high temperatures produce males. The preferred incubation temperature should be between 82 and 88°F (27.8–31.1°C).

When it comes to the selection process, you have lots and lots of choices. Picking the one that's right for you is often a matter of market availability and personal preference.

Exotic Geckos

Madagascar Leaf-tailed Geckos

These magnificent geckos have flattened, leaflike tails. This genus, *Uroplatus*, is endemic to Madagascar. Until the mid-1980s these leaf-tailed geckos were almost unknown in the pet trade. But then the island nation of Madagascar began allowing the export of reptiles and amphibians, and leaf-tailed geckos of not just one but several species became readily available to herpetoculturists. Today (2005) Madagascar has again reversed its policy of animal exportation and relatively few leaf-tailed geckos are imported.

Among the most unusual of the world's gecko species in appearance, the nine species of Madagascan vary in size from only about 4 inches (10 cm) to a full foot (30.5 cm) in length.

Leaf-tails (Henkel's leaf-tail pictured) usually rest head downward on whatever perch they have chosen.

All have well-developed subdigital lamellae and partially webbed toes.

Of the nine species, six currently make their appearance in the pet marketplace, but of those six, only four are seen with any degree of regularity. These geckos can be quite delicate until acclimated to captive conditions. Some are sea level species that are well adapted to warmth; others are denizens of cool, humid, montane forests and languish when subjected to temperatures above 70°F (21.1°C).

Although most of the Madagascan leaf-tails currently on the market are imports, captive breeding successes are becoming more regular. This is good, for many of the imports arrive at dealers severely stressed through hunger and crowding and, most especially, suffering from internal parasites and dehydration. In some cases, placing your gecko into a rain and mist chamber may help the lizard reestablish adequate cell hydration.

To be at their most impressive, Madagascan leaf-tailed geckos must have retained their

sclerophyll forests of that island country. All are long-legged, lanky lizards that, according to species and preferred habitat, are clad in either the hues and patterns of bark or of dead leaves. All members of the genus are relatively slow moving, depending on their wonderful camouflage rather than speed to avoid predators. Even when thermoregulating (head high to a human and in a head down position) on rather exposed tree trunks, these remarkable creatures are all but invisible.

The Giant (or Fringed) Leaf-tailed Gecko

Known scientifically as *Uroplatus fimbriatus*, this impressive, 1-foot long (30.5-cm) gecko is becoming increasingly common in American and European herpetoculture. Skin fringes adorn the sides of the lower jaw, the sides of the body, and the sides of the tail. This is a big brown, brownish gray, or gray lizard that is capable of quite noticeable changes in color intensity and pattern contrast. The eyes—huge, protuberant, and of a weirdly patterned red on silvery gold color—are the only noticeable breaks in the camouflage of this lizard. By night, giant leaf-tails are alert and feed well on large insects; by day, they are quiet to the point of being considered lethargic. This species can tolerate considerable warmth.

Henkel's Leaf-tailed Gecko

Uroplatus henkeli is slightly smaller than the giant leaf-tailed gecko. It is nonetheless an impressive species. The lateral fringes seem less

original tails (something that not many specimens do). In appearance, the original tails are gracefully flattened and bear serrate edges. Regenerated tails are never quite as effectively camouflaged, being in both shape and scalation quite different from the originals.

The various Madagascan leaf-tailed geckos are inhabitants of the remaining rain and damp

The mossy leaf-tailed gecko, **Uroplatus sikorae,** *is another aptly named hobbyist favorite.*

pronounced and *U. henkeli* is capable of assuming an array of colors different from those of *U. fimbriatus.* Additionally, Henkel's leaf-tail seems somewhat hardier than its barely larger cousin.

Despite being rather new to both taxonomists and herpetoculture, Henkel's leaf-tail is now the species most frequently bred by hobbyists. It seems somewhat hardier than the other species and is able to withstand the rigors of extended transportation better than most of its congeners. Although often of bark gray or brown coloration, some individuals rather regularly assume a spectacular banded pattern of lichen gray on charcoal. This is a warmth-tolerant species.

The Mossy Leaf-tailed Gecko

The two subspecies of the 6-inch-long (15-cm) mossy leaf-tail owe their common name to the colors and patterns displayed by most

examples. The subspecies differ in color of the interior of the mouth. *Uroplatus s. sikorae* is known as the white-mouthed mossy leaf-tail while *U. s. sameiti* is referred to as the black-mouthed mossy leaf-tail. The colors of both subspecies of sikorae are those of the ancient trees on which they live—moss green on gray arranged in random lichenate patterns.

A species of relatively high altitudes, the mossy leaf-tails prefer temperatures in the 70 to 75°F (21.1–23.9°C) range with a warmer basking spot. Although difficult, this leaf-tail is now being bred in captivity.

The Satanic Leaf-tailed Gecko

Uroplatus phantasticus is a most remarkable species in an equally remarkable genus. This little (to about 4 to 5 inches [10.2–12.7 cm] in total length) dead-leaf mimic of the higher altitudes (hence cooler temperatures) is sexually

The satanic leaf-tailed gecko, Uroplatus phantasticus, *is a small species of the cooler, higher altitudes of Madagascar.*

below: The spear-point (named for its tail shape) leaf-tailed gecko, Uroplatus ebenaui, *is the smallest species of this genus.*

Despite requiring specialized care, satanic leaf-tailed geckos are readily available.

dimorphic and of variable coloration. Its demonic expression with its pointed eyelids may be viewed against a ground color that ranges from pale lavender to earthen brown.

This is not only one of the less frequently seen species, but is one of the most sought after and expensive as well. When kept cool, the satanic leaf-tailed gecko seems to be rather hardy, eagerly accepting small crickets and wax-worms.

Like other leaf-tails, imported specimens of this wonderfully attractive gecko species often lack their tails entirely or have tails in the initial stages of regeneration. Although this certainly detracts somewhat from their appearance, hobbyists and zoos continue to snap up all specimens offered.

This species has now been captive bred on a number of occasions.

The Spear-point Leaf-tailed Gecko

This, the smallest of the leaf-tails, has an abbreviated spear-point-shaped tail. It is adult at only 3 to 3.5 inches (7.5–8.7 cm) in total length. Known scientifically as *U. ebenaui*, this remains a rarely seen and seldom bred species.

A lined leaf-tailed gecko, **Uroplatus lineatus,** *stalks cautiously through the branches.*

The lined leaf-tailed gecko is slender and long-legged.

The Lined Leaf-tailed Gecko

Uroplatus lineatus is the most atypically marked of the leaf-tailed geckos. Rather than the transverse bars and random lichenate patterns so well displayed by most leaf-tailed geckos, the lined leaf-tail is marked with longitudinal stripes. It is a slender but attractive species that attains 10 inches (25 cm) in total length.

Herpetoculturists are now breeding this species with some regularity, but much about its life history remains enigmatic. It supposedly prefers bamboo and traveler tree forest as habitat.

Note: *Uroplatus alluaudi, U. guentheri,* and *U. peitschmanni* are the three remaining species. They are seldom, if ever, seen in herpetoculture.

Small, rough-scaled, and quiet, the spiny leaf-tailed gecko, **Uroplatus peitschmanni,** *is only seldom available.*

Housing and Nutrition

There are several essential conditions that must be met if you wish to succeed with these interesting leaf-tailed lizards that are being seen with increasing frequency.

1. The proper temperature must be selected and maintained.

2. The cages must be humid but not wet.

3. Healthy stock must initially be procured.

4. Adequate water and an ample and varied diet must be given to the lizards.

The species in this genus are omnivorous, eating saps and other plant exudates as well as insects.

Reproduction

Leaf-tailed geckos of all available species are now being captive bred in increasing numbers. These geckos are easily sexed. Adult males have a decidedly swollen hemipenial area.

Despite the persistently arboreal lifestyles of these geckos, all seem to lay their eggs in the substrate of their cages (or forest floor). The eggs, numbering two per clutch, are nonadhesive and take somewhat less than three months to hatch. Like the adults, the hatchlings are rather slow moving, apparently relying on their marvelous camouflage to avoid detection.

Hatchlings begin accepting fly-sized crickets and houseflies only a day or two after hatching. They grow quickly and within six weeks will graduate to half-grown crickets and waxworms. During this period of rapid growth it is very important to provide the lizards with supplemental calcium and vitamin D_3. Food insects should be dusted at least twice weekly. The hatchlings lapped pendulous droplets after the nightly cage misting.

Although the keeping of these geckos is best reserved for experienced hobbyists, there can be no denying that they are uniquely interesting creatures, well worth all efforts made.

Flying Geckos

The several species of little bark-colored flying geckos of the genus *Ptychozoon* are confusingly similar in appearance. Dark in color, a series of even darker, wavy dorsal markings is usually visible.

Like most geckos, flying geckos can change their color somewhat. Merely variations of a theme, the ground color can lighten or darken, and transverse markings may fade from a strong contrast to near invisibility.

These are wonderful little arboreal geckos with large heads, flattened bodies, lateral skin folds on body and limbs, webbed toes, and

The flying gecko, **Ptychozoon lionatum,** *is a well-camouflaged species.*

scalloped edges on their flattened tails. Although they are utterly incapable of flight, the lateral skin flanges when extended do create a greater surface area that allows the geckos to parachute for fair distances.

When sitting quietly, typically in a head-down position on a tree trunk, these little lizards are virtually invisible. At times, these geckos may even hang inverted on the underside of horizontal limbs. Even when captive and known to be within the confines of a terrarium, flying geckos can be amazingly difficult to find.

There may be as many as five species of flying geckos. Of the five, two species appear rather regularly in the American and European pet trade. These two are *P. lionatum*, which lacks enlarged scales on the dorsum, and *P. kuhlii*, which has enlarged tuberculate scales interspersed among the normal granular dorsal scales.

Most of the specimens available are wild-collected imports.

The lion-tailed flying gecko *P. lionatum* is a little baggy-appearing gecko that may attain an overall length of about 6 inches (15.2 cm). Of this, about half is tail. The sides of original tails are scalloped anteriorly but smooth-sided distally.

Lion-tailed flying geckos are inhabitants of the forested areas of Burma and Thailand. They seem to tolerate the presence of people well and are becoming house geckos in some parts of their range. The have been recently found in Miami, Florida.

Female flying geckos return to chosen deposition sites time and again. The area chosen may be a tree hollow, behind exfoliating bark or rocks, or another such secluded spot. Captive females may even choose a corner angle of their terrarium as a support, gluing the eggs to the glass. The paired eggs have adhesive shells.

Using her hind feet, the female carefully works the eggs into place while the shells are damp and pliable. As the shells dry and solidify, the eggs adhere tightly to their support. At a temperature between 80 and 85°F, the eggs will hatch in about ten weeks.

The hatchlings are nearly 2 inches (5.1 cm) in overall length.

Popular Terrestrial Geckos

The Leopard and Fat-tailed Geckos

The leopard and the fat-tailed geckos are among America's most favored herps. Once familiar with the leopard gecko (*Eublepharis macularius*) and its habits, many hobbyists branch out to a species of similar morphology but very different habits—the fat-tailed gecko (*Hemitheconyx caudicinctus*). This second species remains a very distant runner-up but is gaining new fans with each passing day.

Both of these eublepharine gecko species are now bred in vast numbers in captivity. In fact, captive colonies now produce sufficient numbers of leopard geckos to virtually sustain the demand of hobbyists, and fat-tails are not far behind.

That captive-breeding programs are able to supply the demand for these increasingly popular lizards speaks well not only for the hardiness and adaptability of the geckos, but for the knowledge and diligence of herpetoculturists as well.

Relatives of the leopard and fat-tailed geckos occur in suitable habitats in both North and Central America, Japan, Southeast Asia, and eastern Africa. The most unusual member is *Aeluroscalabotes felinus*, the cat gecko of Southeast Asia. The eublepharines have the caudal (tail) scales arranged in prominent

The cat gecko is known scientifically as **Aeluroscalobotes felinus.**

whorls, and the tails of all are very easily broken. Although they regrow quickly, the regenerated tails differ from the originals in both shape and color. Most often the regenerated tails of the leopard and fat-tailed geckos are turnip-shaped or bulbous in configuration, bear an irregular scalation, and are of a paler color.

Appearance: The natural history of the leopard gecko is much better known than that of the fat-tail. Both, however, are long-lived (15 to 22 years not being uncommon), large-headed, heavy-bodied lizards that are more precisely

patterned and brilliantly colored when young. Leopard geckos are clad in yellows and grays, fat-tails in browns and tans. With increasing age, the striking banded pattern of the baby leopard gecko breaks into a pattern of spots and reticulations. Adult fat-tailed geckos retain the strongly banded pattern of babyhood. A second color phase of the fat-tailed gecko has a broad white middorsal stripe on both head and body. Both tame reasonably well and seem to wear perpetually bemused smiles.

Housing: Because neither leopard nor fat-tailed geckos are overly active, their terrariums can be relatively small. A terrarium made from a 10-gallon (37.9-L) tank is sufficiently large for one male and three females. It should be remembered that fat-tailed geckos are capable of withstanding slightly more humid conditions than those preferred by leopard geckos. In fact, a slightly higher relative humidity may even be beneficial to the former.

The substrate for both species may consist of 1 to 2 inches (2.5–5.1 cm) of sand, small pebbles, cypress mulch, or other such material. The use of sharp-edged silica aquarium gravel is

Albino leopard geckos are now readily available.

contraindicated, for intestinal impaction may occur if the lizard accidentally ingests any substantial amount while feeding. Several cork bark or similar hiding places should be provided for these nocturnal lizards. A low receptacle of clean water should always be present.

Diet: By nature, eublepharine geckos feed upon living insects and other arthropods. For captives, crickets, common and giant mealworms, waxworms, butterworms, and other such commonly available insects are all excellent food items. Newly born (pinkie) mice are also eagerly accepted by many, if not most, larger gecko specimens. A varied diet is better than a constant one, and the size of the food items must be tailored to the size of your lizards.

If neither yard nor garden insecticides are used, an even more variable diet can be offered your lizards. Not only are such things as sow bugs and hairless caterpillars relished by geckos, but wild insects generally contain more nutrition than domestically raised ones. If store-purchased insects are the exclusive food of your lizards, be certain to dust them liberally with a calcium and vitamin D_3 supplement. This is especially important during periods of rapid

Spotted when young, leucistic leopard geckos lose their pattern as they age.

growth or egg production, when juveniles and females, respectively, will require larger than normal amounts of calcium for healthy bone formation and eggshell production.

Prey acquisition: The hunting strategy of eublepharine geckos is both interesting and, at times, comical. The approach by the lizard to a food item may be either stealthy or darting, and is often accompanied by an accentuated amount of tail-writhing and posturing. The final grasping of the food item is rapid and sure. Mastication is thorough.

Reproduction—Sexing: Most of the leopard and fat-tailed geckos offered by the pet trade are of juvenile to subadult size. (Of the two, the

Herpetoculturists are striving to develop an African fat-tailed gecko, Hemitheconyx caudicinctus, even blacker than this example.

leopard gecko seems to grow slightly faster, often attaining sexual maturity in slightly less than a year.)

Adults may be easily sexed by comparing the areas immediately anterior and posterior to the cloacal opening (anus). To do so, it will be necessary to grasp your lizard (firmly yet gently) and turn it upside down. Males, especially those that are sexually active, have a vaguely chevron-shaped (apex anterior) series of enlarged preanal pores as well as a proportionately bulbous tail base. The bulbosity is formed by the hemipenes. These characteristics are lacking on females.

An albino African fat-tailed gecko.

Sex is determined by incubation temperature, rather than genetically.

Ideally, incubation should be accomplished at a temperature of from 84 to 86°F (28.9–30°C). Within this rather narrow temperature range, both sexes will be produced (see chart, page 57).

Adult behavior: Male eublepharine geckos are highly territorial. No more than a single male may be kept to each cage, but usually several females may be kept with him.

Occasionally, even the females can be aggressive, and until your colony is established it will be necessary to monitor the activities of all. If severely subordinate, a lizard may refuse food and soon succumb.

Breeding: Although the breeding season for your geckos may vary slightly according to your latitude, it usually encompasses a seven- or eight-month period that begins in late autumn or early winter. Some breeders precondition their geckos by cooling them to about 70°F [21.1°C] days and 60°F [15.6°C] nights) for the month of October while others claim this to be unnecessary. Except for the cooling period a heat tape is activated beneath one end of the gecko's terrariums both day and night. A natural photoperiod is provided throughout the year.

Like leopard geckos, African fat-tails are now available in many colors and patterns. This is a striped normal.

Food is reduced while the geckos are cooled but is increased when they are again warmed. The geckos are allowed to eat until sated (thin lizards will produce fewer, weaker eggs). An egg-deposition area, such as a low 2-inch (5.1-cm) margarine cup containing barely moistened sand or vermiculite, can be nestled into the sand near one corner. Seldom would the female fail to use this. The eggs are removed on the morning following deposition and placed in a temperature-controlled Styrofoam incubator.

Incubation: A healthy female eublepharine gecko should produce several clutches of two eggs each over the breeding season. Incubation duration varies with temperature (shorter when warmer), but will probably average about 55 days. A number of incubation media are successfully used. Among others are sphagnum, peat, sand, perlite, and vermiculite. See pages 44–45 for suggestions on egg incubation.

Because they are hardy and easily cared for, both leopard and fat-tailed geckos are ideal lizards for beginners. The fact that they are attractive and prolific adds an extra dimension of enjoyment to their maintenance.

The Frog-eyed Geckos

Several species of frog-eyed geckos are occasionally available in the pet trade. The greater frog-eye (*Teratoscincus scincus scincus*) is among these. It is a robust gecko and is adult at between 4.5 and 6.25 inches (11.4–15.9 cm) in total length.

A wide-ranging species, the greater frog-eyed gecko can be encountered in desert and other arid-land habitats from southern Asia (including southern areas of the former U.S.S.R.) to western China and many mideastern countries, and on to Pakistan. This species is an excellent digger, excavating its burrows down through the dry surface sands well into the moister subsurface sands. The desert areas in which this Asian gecko dwells are subject to definite day and night, as well as seasonal, temperature changes. These temperature extremes should be considered when housing the species as captives.

These vocal geckos are crepuscular and nocturnal as well as seasonal in their activity patterns. Winter cold can bring about rather extended periods of brumation. They are, however, active throughout the warmer seasons of

Frog-eyed geckos (this is Teratoscincus s. scincus*) have a very delicate, easily torn skin.*

the year. Their sharp call notes denote both territoriality and anger (the two not being awfully distantly removed).

But unlike other geckos, frog-eyes have a secondary method of producing sounds. When the tail is writhed, as it is when the greater frog-eyed gecko becomes defensive (or otherwise excited), a scraping sound is produced. This is caused by the large supracaudal scales (the scales on the top of the tail) rubbing together.

Appearance: Frog-eyed geckos are clad in scales of earthen hues. The dorsal background coloration may be yellowish or buff. Against this are darker and lighter spots or broken stripes. The sides are pale and the venter is immaculate white. The scales of the head are small. Those of the trunk (including venter), limbs, and tail are noticeably enlarged and fishlike (cycloid), with the scales along the top of the tail being the very largest. The head of this gecko species is broad but somewhat foreshortened. The eyes are prominently large and rimmed with scales that serve as eyelashes. The limbs are long and powerfully

built. Rather than expanded climbing lamellae, the geckos of this genus have a fringe of comb-like scales along their toes. These scales permit greater ease of motion in fine-sand habitats. This gecko is also an accomplished burrower.

The skin of all species of frog-eyed geckos is very delicate and permeable. It can be easily torn if the gecko squirms while being handled. The tail is remarkably easily autotomized, at times being broken with what seems merely a touch. If your gecko is healthy, the skin will heal and the tail will regenerate. However, both problems (and especially the first) are stressful for the animal. I suggest that the members of this genus be cupped (directed into a jar or glass) so that they can be moved without actually being restrained in the hand.

Housing: The very thin skin of the members of the genus *Teratoscincus* does little to inhibit desiccation. The thin integument is extensively vascularized, readily allowing gas and moisture exchange. It is for this reason that these geckos burrow through the dry surface layers of sand

and terminate their burrows in the moister sub-surface areas. If their terrarium is set up in a like manner, *Teratoscincus* will thrive.

To even come close to accomplishing this will require several inches of sand substrate. I suggest a minimum of 8 inches (20.3 cm), with from 12 to 14 inches (30.5–35.6 cm) being much better. To moisten the bottom layers of sand without saturating the top ones will require the insertion of a small-diameter standpipe or some rocks on one end of the terrarium that reach from the bottom to above the level of the top of the sand. A small amount of water poured into the pipe or in the fissures in the rocks will flow directly into the bottom layers of sand without wetting the top. If an earthen (clay) pipe of suitable diameter is used, it can serve dual purposes. Tilted so that it provides easy ingress and egress, besides serving as a water conduit, it provides the geckos a daytime hiding area.

The weight of the sand in a frog-eyed gecko terrarium can be considerable. Care should be given that the terrarium has been placed in its permanent location before the sand is added and dampened, and that the stand on which the terrarium is placed is sturdy enough to hold the weight.

A pair of frog-eyed sand geckos can be housed in a terrarium having a floor space of about 12 × 30 inches (30.5 × 76.2 cm). Daytime temperatures of 84 to 94°F (28.9–34.4°C) in localized areas—not the entire terrarium—that can reach slightly higher temperatures for short periods of time are best. The deep sand substrate can be warmed from beneath by the prudent use of heat tapes and heating pads and from above by heat lamps. It is important that a thermal gradient be provided, with the sand at one end of the tank being cooler than that at the other. This will allow your geckos to choose the sand temperature at which they feel most comfortable. The entire terrarium should be allowed to cool by 10 to 15°F (5.6–8.4°C) at night.

Feeding: During the warm months of summer, frog-eyed geckos should be fed often. They should be fat and healthy prior to the winter cooling that is to follow. The winter cooling period should last from five to eight weeks. During that period daytime highs of 60 to 65°F (15.6–18.3°C) and nighttime lows of 50 to 60°F (10–15.6°C) will suffice. This will condition the lizards for breeding.

It is likely that the lizards will become entirely inactive and remain in their burrows during this cooling period. Food will be unnecessary during this period. It is because of this fasting that it is so necessary that your geckos be in excellent health and have good body weight prior to cooling. Care must be taken that the sand substrate not be allowed to dry out during this period of semi-brumation. Also keep a surface water dish available and filled at all times.

The diet of this gecko in the wild consists largely of beetles. Captives will eat mealworms

A lesser frog-eyed gecko, **Teratolepis microlepis.**

and their beetles, giant mealworms and their beetles, crickets, grasshoppers (not lubbers, which are variably toxic), and other nonnoxious beetles. Some specimens will also accept newly born mice.

Behavior: Frog-eyed geckos can be cannibalistic, consuming lizards of other species as well as their own hatchlings. Properly conditioned female frog-eyed geckos will deposit several clutches of two (rarely one) hard-shelled but very easily damaged eggs during the summer months. Quite unlike the eggs of most other gecko species that require a high humidity, the eggs of the frog-eyed sand geckos do not. Preferred humidity is in the 40 to 55 percent range. At 80 to 90°F (26.7–32.2°C), the incubation period will be from 70 to 100 days. The moisture content and humidity in the incubation medium that would be normal for other species can prove fatal to the developing embryos of *Teratoscincus*.

This species is not yet being captive bred in large numbers. Most of the specimens currently being offered in the pet trade are wild-caught imports.

Hatchlings of this species are much more brilliantly colored than the adults, being a rather bright yellow with black crossbands.

Collectively, frog-eyed geckos are among the more aggressive (defensive?) gecko species. Their defense posture is stylized and interesting. When approached by a predator (or your hand) the frog-eyed gecko assumes a tiptoe stance, mouth open, throat (gular) area expanded, back humped, and tail writhing. If the threat continues, the gecko will squeak, dart toward the object, deliver a slicing bite, then turn and dart to its burrow, into which it will dash headlong if allowed.

Although they may be somewhat more demanding than many geckos in their terrarium needs, frog-eyed sand geckos are very interesting and well worth the extra effort required.

You will need to heed the handling cautions delineated earlier in this account. The probability of your specimens sustaining torn skin and tail loss during what you might consider a routine procedure must always be a very real concern.

Not all of the members of the genus *Teratoscincus* have enlarged fishlike scales. The somewhat smaller species, *T. microlepis*, often called the "lesser frog-eyed gecko," is clad in small granular scales. This very attractive lizard may be successfully maintained in the manner just discussed.

The Web-footed Sand Gecko

The web-footed sand gecko (*Palmatogecko rangei*) is a specialized sand swimmer endemic to the fog-shrouded Namib Desert in southwestern Africa. There, it dwells among the ever-changing dunes of this strangely complex and unique habitat.

Appearance: Besides being of slender build, the web-footed gecko is a small gecko species, attaining only a 4-inch (10.2-cm) overall length. *Palmatogecko* is a persistently nocturnal species that is active throughout the year when climatic conditions are suitable.

Males produce clicks and squeaks, both during territorial displays and when restrained.

The web-footed gecko is clad in finely granular scales similar in color to those of the sands on which it dwells. Tans, buffs, and the palest of grays are the usual hues. The two most unusual external characteristics are the feet and the eyes of this species. The toes are webbed to their tips with a thin pliable skin. This gives the lizard the appearance of wearing snowshoes. The eyes are very large and protuberant. The iris of each is colored in dark and red pigments that are especially apparent in well-lit situations when the vertical pupils are tightly contracted.

Habitat: The coastal Namibian desert is one of the world's most unusual habitats. Because of the proximity of cold austral ocean currents to the coast, this desert is often shrouded in dense fogs. It is also different from most deserts in that it has minimal daytime and nighttime temperature differences. This, then, is the home of *Palmatogecko rangei*, and it is these conditions that you must strive to duplicate if you hope to keep the web-footed gecko successfully in the terrarium.

As a result of the persistent fogs in this desert habitat, some moisture often exists beneath the surface of the sands. It is within this layer of slight moisture that the geckos construct their home burrows. This is not a habitat easily duplicated in the home terrarium, but is the one for which you are striving.

Housing: See the captive-care suggestions for the frog-eyed gecko, pages 70–71, for terrarium setup procedures. A few flat rocks (such as pieces of shale) and drought-tolerant plants (sansevierias or haworthias) can be provided for cage furniture. Pieces of cork bark and the bleached, hollowed skeletons of opuntia (cholla) cactus can also be supplied but are not absolutely necessary.

It should be remembered that, although web-footed geckos are desert dwellers, they construct rather deep burrows to escape the worst of the heat. In the terrarium daytime temperatures of between 88 to 95°F (31.1–35°C) on the sand surface are suitable. The below-surface temperature should be somewhat cooler.

Nighttime temperatures should be allowed to drop by only a few degrees, if at all. Web-footed geckos will drink water from flat receptacles, but

The webbed feet of **Palmatogecko rangei** *help in its movements across loose desert sand.*

also will lap the droplets from the rocks in their terrarium if these are misted during the gecko's period of activity. Web-footed geckos prefer prey insects of small size and are especially fond of termites and baby crickets. These geckos have a reputation for being delicate captives.

Although it is true that they prefer rather exact terrarium conditions, when these conditions are met, and when adequately small food insects are provided in sufficient quantity, this is a hardy species.

As with all geckos, to prevent aggression, no more than a single male should be kept in each terrarium. From one to several females may be housed with each male. Successful captive breedings of the web-footed sand gecko have recently been reported.

The Helmeted Gecko

Appearance: The helmeted gecko (*Geckonia chazaliae*) has only recently become available to American herpetoculture. Although only 3.5 inches (8.9 cm) in length when adult, it is big-headed and robust.

Geckonia chazaliae has a circlet of enlarged scales from which its common name of helmeted gecko is derived.

Habitat: The arid-land dwelling helmeted gecko hails from North Africa. It seems to prefer rocky and gravelly areas. Weather permitting, *Geckonia* is active year-round. It is capable of brumating for short periods if necessary.

Both crepuscular and nocturnal in nature, captives may also forage by day, especially when in reduced light situations.

The vocalizations of the helmeted gecko are low-pitched clicks with little carrying power.

Appearance: This desert and dry savanna gecko is clad in earthen-colored scales. The background color can vary from reddish buff to pale gray. Dark and/or light markings may or may not be present. The scalation is irregular and variably tuberculate. The common name is derived from the row of large conical scales at the rear of the head. The head is proportionately large and the large, heavily browed eyes are lidless. The legs are sturdy, the toes short, flattened, serrate laterally, and webbed basally.

Behavior: *Geckonia* is an interesting and normally slow-moving little lizard. When startled it may move in short bursts of speed. A trio will thrive in a 15-gallon (56.8 L) capacity terrarium.

The substrate can be sand over which is strewn an ample scattering of pea- to penny-sized chipped rocks. When still, the little geckos with their variable color and variably sized and roughened scales can be nearly invisible against this background.

This gecko species is quite hardy and undemanding. Heat tapes provide daytime temperatures of 85 to 96°F (29.4–35.6°C). Turn the tapes off in the evening, allowing nighttime temperatures to drop into the 70s°F (20s°C). For one month during the winter, drop temperatures an additional 10°F (5.6°C).

Diet: Helmeted geckos drink readily from a low water dish when thirsty but really seem to need little moisture. Those I have had have preferred slow, crawling prey to fast-moving crickets, but after a time would readily eat nearly any insects offered. They were fed sparingly during the month-long period of winter cooling.

Reproduction: Helmeted geckos are being bred both in the United States and in Europe on a regular but sparing basis. At 86°F (30°C), the eggs hatch in about 70 days. The only female I have had that produced eggs delivered three clutches at about 23-day intervals. One egg from each clutch was infertile.

A Madagascar ocelot gecko, Paroedura pictus, *in its terrarium.*

"Cute"—a word not regularly applied to reptiles—is the term often applied to these unique little lizards. The availability of *Geckonia* varies month by month and year by year. At some times they are so readily available that the prices drop to near $50 each. At other times, helmeted geckos may command three times that much or not be available at all.

Although I consider this species rather easily kept, it displays just enough idiosyncrasies to be challenging. Therefore, it is best suited for experienced hobbyists.

The Ocelot Gecko

The ocelot gecko (*Paroedura pictus*) is a small denizen of arid-land and rocky savanna habitats of western, southern, and eastern Madagascar.

An adult size of 5 inches (12.7 cm) is attained. Males may be slightly the larger of the two sexes. Adults are largely terrestrial, but hatchlings and juveniles climb rather agilely.

The ocelot gecko is a nocturnal species that is active during all but the very coldest times of the the year.

Male ocelot geckos are capable of producing "clicks" and "squeaks." They are vocal during the breeding season, at which times territoriality and sexual dominance is at its peak.

Because of the tropical latitudes at which the ocelot gecko is found, breeding activity may actually occur over much of the year.

Appearance: The ocelot gecko occurs in two distinct color and pattern phases. The first is banded with creamish gray against a ground color of deep brown (with advancing age the bands weaken and diffuse into numerous spots). The second phase lacks all but vestiges of bands, bearing instead a prominent light mid-dorsal stripe.

Hatchlings and juveniles are somewhat more brilliantly colored and precisely patterned than the adults. Both dorsal and lateral surfaces bear prominently tuberculate scales. The head is large, the body slender. The developing eggs can be seen as diffuse light areas through the lateral and ventral body walls of the female. Each toe is tipped with two leaflike pads.

Behavior: Despite being agile and fast, this attractive little gecko is not overly active; a pair or trio may be maintained and bred in a 10-gallon-capacity (37.9-L) terrarium. A 2-inch (5.1-cm) bottom substrate of peat and sand mixture will allow the females to nest naturally. If the terrarium is misted regularly, the slight moisture buildup in the substrate will provide a suitable incubation medium for the eggs. At a temperature of between 83 and 86°F (28.3–30°C), the incubation time will be a day or two less

This juvenile ocelot gecko has not yet begun to assume the diffused pattern of adulthood.

or more than two months. If you prefer not to have a substrate such as described here, you can use an indoor/outdoor carpet and provide a shallow 4 × 4-inch (10.2-cm²) plastic dish with 1 inch (2.5 cm) of barely moistened laying medium. The female will seek this out for deposition of her eggs. Pieces of cork bark or other such areas of seclusion must be provided.

Ocelot geckos are both attractive and hardy. Although some are bred by hobbyists, most offered in the pet marketplace are imported specimens.

Diet: Ocelot geckos feed readily on half-grown crickets, waxworms, and other similarly sized insect fare. They will drink water from a flat dish. Food insects should be dusted with a vitamin D3 and calcium supplement at least once weekly.

These are a tropical species that prefers daytime temperatures of 82 to 88°F (27.8–31.1°C). A drop of several degrees at night is perfectly acceptable.

Breeding: Breeding is probably stimulated by a slight lengthening in the photoperiod as well as by increasing humidity. Because this is a Southern Hemisphere species, ocelot geckos

may take a season or two to acclimate to the reversed seasons of the Northern Hemisphere.

These pretty and interesting geckos are deserving of consideration by any hobbyist. They are easy enough to keep and breed to be considered a beginner's species. Ocelot geckos tolerate handling rather well.

Hatchling Madagascar ocelot geckos, *Paroedura pictus,* are much more brilliantly marked than the adults.

The Day Geckos of Madagascar

The genus *Phelsuma* contains approximately 60 species of geckos that, because of their propensities for daytime (as well as nighttime) activities, are usually referred to as "day geckos." For the most part restricted to Madagascar and surrounding islands, representatives of the genus also occur in the Seychelles, in the Comoros, on the islands of Réunion and Mauritius, and on Round Island. A few have become established in Hawaii and in Florida. A single species occurs on the Andaman Islands in India's Bay of Bengal. Two large species, both now extinct, once occurred on the island of Rodriguez.

The blue-tailed day gecko, **Phelsuma cepediana,** *is a beautiful species of Mauritius and Madagascar. It is of moderate size.*

The name "day gecko," although not entirely descriptive, does acknowledge that these wonderfully attractive geckos are active during the daylight hours when most other gecko species are quietly resting.

However, the common name fails to call attention to the fact that day geckos are also active well into the hours of darkness.

Appearance: The day geckos range in size from small (3 inches [7.6 cm]) to large (12 inches [30.5 cm]) with most being somewhere between these two sizes.

All have expanded digital disks and lidless eyes bearing round pupils, and most have a green (or at least greenish) ground color (a very few are brown or gray). Day geckos are omnivorous, consuming not only insects but pollen, nectar, overripe fruits, and saps and juices as well.

Of the (about) 60 extant species of *Phelsuma*, several are critically imperiled because of continuing habitat degradation.

A portrait of a hatchling Madagascar giant day gecko.

Although they were once considered difficult captives, in recent years more thorough understanding of their needs has proven many species of day geckos to be hardy and long-lived.

Important: Day geckos are extremely territorial. Unless your caging facilities are of the walk-in or enclosed atrium size, you should not attempt to keep more than a single male and two or three females per terrarium. It is best if all geckos housed in a single enclosure are of a similar size and are introduced to their new quarters simultaneously. Even then, a hierarchy will quickly be established.

Small Species

Neon (Yellow-headed) Day Gecko

Appearance: *Phelsuma klemmeri* is a newly discovered form of remarkable beauty. The yellow of the head is actually a chartreuse or a lime green. The dorsum is turquoise anteriorly and olive-tan posteriorly. The tail is turquoise, brightest distally. The limbs are olive tan, obscurely peppered with lighter pigment. A broad black lateral line is present from tympanum to groin. This is bordered beneath by the white of the venter. The surface of the head is peppered with tiny black speckles; two blue dots, one in the black post-tympanal stripe and one immediately anterior to the shoulder, are present.

This tiny, flattened day gecko attains a 3-inch (7.6-cm) overall length. *Phelsuma klemmeri* is found in coastal northwestern Madagascar, where it dwells on large, rough-barked trees, retreating into bark crevices and hollows when threatened. The flattened conformation stands this species in good stead for such retreat and dictates that *P. klemmeri* be maintained in absolutely escape-proof terrariums. These little lizards are able to sidle into and escape through the slightest apertures.

Reproduction: Although this species is not considered an egg-gluer, females may place their eggs high in leaf sheaths of bamboo as well as inside the hollows of bamboo stems. They will adhere to such surfaces but are easily dislodged.

Feeding: Fly-sized crickets, termites, springtails, flightless fruit flies, and day gecko formula are all readily consumed.

Behavior: Yellow-headed day geckos are hardy and easily bred—but caution! If you think the adults are escape artists, just wait until a 1-inch-long (2.5-cm) hatchling demonstrates its prowess at escape.

Neon day geckos are now seldom imported and few breeding programs include them. This, and the fact that they are so beautiful, rather assures that the asking price will remain high in the foreseeable future.

This female neon day gecko is gravid.

Medium-size Species

Gold-dust Day Gecko

Appearance: Although the specific scientific name, *P. laticauda*, refers to a flattail, this common name is more generally applied to the somewhat larger *P. serraticauda*, a species with not only a flattened but a flanged tail as well. The more accepted common name of gold-dust day gecko refers to the liberal peppering of yellow on the nape and shoulder area.

The gold-dust day gecko is usually a brilliant green species that often displays a bluish tinge ventrolaterally and on the limbs and feet. Some specimens may display a yellowish wash on their dorsal surface. A trio of elongated, orange teardrop markings adorn the mid-dorsum. These are followed posteriorly by a varying number of smaller orange markings that may be discrete or coalesce into a vaguely reticulate pattern. This is a 5-inch-long (12.7-cm) species.

The common name of gold-dust day gecko is now used for **Phelsuma laticauda.** *Inset: The gold-flecking on the gold-dust day gecko is most profuse anteriorly.*

The gold-dust day gecko is widely distributed. It not only occurs on Madagascar, but on the Comoro Islands as well, and has been introduced into the Seychelles, Hawaii, and Florida. *Phelsuma laticauda* is a hardy and easily bred species. The eggs are easily incubated, and the hatchlings are about 1.5 inches (3.8 cm) in overall length.

Laticauda readily consumes both insect prey and gecko formula.

Peacock Day Gecko

Appearance: In my estimation *P. quadriocellata* is one of the most beautiful of the day geckos. The specific name of "quadriocellata" translates literally to "four spots." The three subspecies are found along much of the eastern

A peacock day gecko removes adhering bits of shedding skin from its toes.

coast of Madagascar. The leaf-green dorsum is peppered anteriorly with turquoise. A blue chevron often appears on the snout, its apex above the nostrils. The dorsum is variably marked with orange dots and dashes from the shoulders to the anterior tail. A pair of turquoise-outlined black spots are present posterior to the forelimbs. A dark marking (usually not actually a spot) is present immediately anterior to each hind limb.

This is basically an arboreal species that commonly attains a rather robust 4.5-inch (11.4-cm) overall length.

Another aggressive species, it may be necessary to separate males from females except for breeding interludes.

Reproduction: The eggs of the peacock day gecko are moderately adhesive when freshly laid. Those laid in the hollows of cut bamboo are usually rather well secured; those affixed to yielding leaves are more easily dislodged.

The hatchlings are just a little over 1 inch (2.5 cm) in length when emerging from the paired eggs. Although preferring high humidity, peacock day geckos are hardy and can be prolific breeders if properly cycled.

Large Species

Giant Day Gecko

In one or another of its four subspecies, the large, attractive *P. madagascariensis* is the hands-down favorite day gecko among hobbyists. It is the only one of the day geckos that the dealers routinely designate by subspecies. All of the four subspecies have been bred extensively in captivity, with most emphasis seemingly placed on the subspecies *grandis* and *madagascariensis.*

Courtship is aggressive, and many visual barriers and plenty of space are necessary to prevent the females from being injured by the larger males.

The giant day gecko is highly arboreal, and as such does best in heavily planted, vertically oriented terrariums or the large wood and wire walk-in cages described earlier (see page 20).

Reproduction: Egg-laying females orient themselves nearly vertically between the leaves of stiff-leafed plants such as sansevierias, bananas, or, in captivity, bromeliads. They lay an egg, hold it in the rear feet until the shell has dried, place the egg deep in the axils of the plant in which they are positioned, then repeat

Boehme's day gecko, **Phelsuma madagascariensis boehmei,** *is pretty, large, and rather uncommon in the hobby.*

the process with the second of the two-egg clutch. The eggs are nonadhesive and can be easily removed to an incubator.

This is (arguably) the largest of Madagascar's day geckos. The largest examples of the largest subspecies attain 1 foot (30.5 cm) in length.

Diet: All subspecies will eagerly accept suitably sized insect prey and avidly consume their gecko formula. The subspecies of the giant day gecko are:

• Boehm's Giant Day Gecko, *P. m. boehmi*, is restricted in distribution to the central eastern coast of Madagascar. The largest markings are in the forms of dots and dashes on the dorsal surface of the head. A broad ocular stripe is present, beginning above the tympanum and converging on the tip of the snout. Numerous orange dots and short dashes are present over most of the dorsum. The lateral scales are prominent and noticeably tuberculate. Adults are somewhat less than 9 inches (22.9 cm) in length. This is not a commonly offered race of giant day gecko.

Ornate day geckos are small, hardy, and very attractive.

This subspecies of the Madagascar giant day gecko is **Phelsuma m. madagascariensis.**

• Madagascar Giant Day Gecko, *P. m. grandis*, adults regularly exceed a 10-inch (25.4-cm) length and seem to top out at about 1 foot (30.5 cm). Males attain a larger size than the females. This is a bright green subspecies with prominent maroon head markings and equally prominent (usually), well-defined orange dorsal markings. Occasionally, some blue is present, especially on the sides of the head. The amount of orange present seems to vary individually, and cannot be used as a characteristic to determine geographic origin of the lizard. These are remarkably impressive geckos. This remains an abundant race that is widely spread in northern Madagascar and on the surrounding islands.

• Koch's Giant Day Gecko, *P. m. kochi*, is usually a rather uniform kelly green. It has scales that are prominently tuberculate on the sides and jowls. The orange highlights, so prominent on the other three races, are greatly reduced in intensity. This race occurs in western and northwestern Madagascar. It is highly arboreal, but often suns while positioning itself head downward on the trunk of a tree. Although usually about 9 inches (22.9 cm) in overall length, this race can attain an imposing 12 inches (30.5 cm).

• Madagascar Day Gecko, *P. m. madagascariensis*, is smaller than *grandis* (note that the word "giant" is omitted from the common name of this 9-inch-long [22.9-cm] race). It ranges widely in eastern Madagascar as well as some of the eastern islands. A population also exists near the southeastern city of Taolonaro. A maroon ocular stripe is usually present. The orange spots on the dorsal surface of the head are usually only weakly defined. The green of the dorsum can be variable, ranging from light to dark green. The orange spots of the dorsum are often arranged in three weakly defined longitudinal rows, the vertebral row being the best defined. The lateral scales are tuberculate, those of the jowls prominently so.

• Standing's day gecko, *P. standingi*, is the second of the two contenders for Madagascar's largest day gecko species. Standing's day gecko, large and grayish green or bluish green when adult, is prominently banded with russet and blue-gray when hatched. Adult males attain 1 foot (30.5 cm) in length. Females are marginally smaller.

This is a heavy-bodied, very impressive species. Although lacking the brilliance of the earlier species, Standing's day geckos display a subtle beauty in their coloration. Until recently, Standing's day geckos have been infrequently seen in

The beautiful colors of hatchling Standing's geckos, **Phelsuma standingi,** *fade to pale green with growth.*

the pet trade. Now that this species from arid southwestern Madagascar is seen more regularly in the pet trade, concern is being voiced about its well-being in the wild. It seems that not only are the animals being collected, but their habitat is besieged by the charcoal trade as well. When properly cared for, Standing's day geckos have lived for more than 15 years as captives.

Ours are kept in a large walk-in cage on the side deck. These lizards have time and again experienced nighttime temperatures in the high 30s and low 40s°F (0–7°C) with no signs of distress.

They quickly access their basking perches with the rising of the sun and are soon foraging for crickets, giant mealworms, and the gecko formula. Although this trio of Standing's geckos are quite compatible, new adult specimens are quickly set upon by both the male and the two females, even in the large, well planted walk-in cage in which they now reside. Little or no attention is given by the adults to juveniles, but when sexual maturity is reached they are mercilessly badgered, necessitating removal.

Stress: Day geckos kept too cool, too crowded, or too hot, or subjected to aggression

Phelsuma guimbeaui, *the orange-spotted day gecko, is now established in Hawaii.*

by dominant terrarium mates will display certain signs of stress. Among these are a tendency for the subordinate specimen(s) to continually hide, to lack a feeding response, to be continually fearful and nervous, and to persistently display an abnormal coloration (usually dark).

Stress can prove fatal to an otherwise healthy gecko. Observe your day geckos frequently and get to know what are, for yours, normal colors and responses. Certain species are more aggressive toward tankmates than others.

Stress may be reduced by adding visual barriers, by placing your animals in a larger cage, by adjusting cage temperature, or by adding additional females. If, after all of these corrective measures, stress continues, you will have no choice but to separate your specimens into individual terrariums.

If this becomes necessary, it is usually possible to periodically move the male to the female's container for the purpose of breeding. Watch carefully for signs of overt aggressiveness toward the female by the male. It may be necessary to again separate the two almost immediately.

If relatively compatible, it still may be necessary to again separate the two after breeding has been accomplished. Observe and be ready to take whatever steps are necessary.

Housing: Because of their remarkable brilliance and small size, most day geckos are ideal candidates for inclusion in the tropical woodland terrarium. The size of the terrariums should be dictated by the adult size of the day geckos retained therein.

Because they are persistently arboreal, day geckos do best in a tall terrarium.

Day geckos do not tolerate crowding well. For a pair or trio of small to moderately sized geckos, a 15-gallon (56.8-L) tall tank will provide sufficient space. For a pair or trio of the large species, a terrarium ranging in size from 30 gallons (113.6 L) (minimum) to 80 gallons (302.8 L) is best.

If constrained too tightly, day geckos may survive but won't thrive. If indoors, the terrarium should boast full-spectrum lighting. A full-spectrum incandescent bulb will provide warmth as well as illumination. A large hollow log, a few cross branches of bamboo, and a wildly clambering *Epipremnum aureum* (pothos or variegated philodendron) will provide security, visual barriers, a feeding platform, and multiple drinking stations.

To provide drinking water for the lizards, the leaves of the plant may be misted daily with tepid water. A substrate of several inches of sterilized potting soil will suffice.

Eggs may be placed on the substrate, inside the hollow log, or on the plants. From there, the eggs are easily gathered and incubated.

Some Terrarium Basics

Perches: Both horizontal and vertical perches are necessary to the well-being of day geckos. Illuminate and warm at least one of the horizontal perches (preferably two) to provide a suitable basking area for your geckos. Sections of bamboo are ideal perch material. Tank-length sections can be held in place by a dollop of Silicone aquarium sealant on each end.

Visual barriers: If you are keeping more than a single day gecko per terrarium, visual barriers are desired and may even be imperative to prevent intraspecific aggression. The adage "out of sight, out of mind" aptly applies here. The visual barriers can be provided by utilizing a crisscross of bamboo lengths, a suitably sized vining plant, or a combination of the two.

Water: Day geckos prefer to drink by lapping pendulous droplets of water from freshly misted plant leaves or bamboo sections. Many day geckos will steadfastly refuse to drink from a water dish. Mist the leaves of your plants with

A Homemade Artificial Diet for Your Day Geckos

1/3 jar of mixed fruit or apricot strained baby food
1/3 jar of strained papaya baby food
1 teaspoon of honey
1/3 eyedropper of Avitron liquid bird vitamins
1/2 teaspoon of Osteoform powdered vitamins

Add water to a proper soupy consistency.
Occasionally when I have bee pollen available, I add a small amount. The geckos do not seem to care, either way.
Refrigerate between uses. Check to make sure this does not sour or ferment in the refrigerator.

tepid water daily. Be certain that the plants you use have not been freshly sprayed with insecticides or liquid fertilizers.

Plants: Grow commercially procured plants for a couple of weeks outside of the terrarium to allow systemic additives a chance to dissipate. To grow in a terrarium, plants (even forest plants) will need strong lighting. Incandescent fixtures using commercial plant-grow floodlight bulbs are ideal. These bulbs will provide warmth for your geckos as well as the necessary illumination for the plants. In addition, either incandescent or fluorescent full-spectrum bulbs should be used. This will provide small amounts of ultraviolet (UV-A and UV-B) rays for your geckos. These UV rays assist reptiles in properly metabolizing vitamins and minerals and in promoting natural behavior by the lizards.

Nutrition: As mentioned earlier, day geckos have complex (but, fortunately, rather easily duplicated) diets. They not only consume

An Ideal Phelsuma Caging Facility

You should provide as much room as possible for any captive reptiles. An easily cleaned wire-covered wood-frame cage of almost walk-in size is ideal for the day geckos.

The top and bottom of the cage are made of 0.75-inch (19.1-mm) exterior plywood. The center of the top has been removed, leaving only a 6-inch-wide (15.2-cm) rim all around. I have found this approach gives greater stability than a top framed in with 2 × 2-inch (5.1 × 5.1-cm) lumber. The uprights and door are made from carefully chosen, straight, pressure-treated 2 × 2-inch (5.1 × 5.1-cm) lumber.

The wire is 0.125-inch (3.2-mm) mesh hardware cloth (this size will retain all but the smallest crickets). The whole cage is mounted on large casters to facilitate easy moving.

Suggested dimensions: 6 feet (1.8 m) high (including casters) by 4 feet (1.2 m) long, just narrow enough to fit through interior doors. The dimensions of the hinged door are 24 (width) × 48 (height) inches (61 × 122 cm).

The wire is fastened to the frame using stainless staples 0.75 inch (19.1 mm) long from a standard staple gun. Those that don't fit tightly are tapped in with a hammer. A potted ficus tree is placed within, and several sizable branches provide additional perches.

Vining philodendron clambers across the bottom. For cleaning, the cage is rolled outside and hosed down thoroughly. The cage remains out on a sunny deck from mid-spring to late autumn. It is brought out on suitable days all year long. During the winter, 4-mil plastic sheeting is stapled over the wire on three sides and the top to lessen the cool breezes and concentrate the heat from the winter sun.

insects, but seek out nectars, pollens, exudates from overripe fruits and the fruits themselves, and plant saps as well.

The fondness of day geckos for sweet fruit and flower by-products offers you a simple way of administering the necessary vitamin and mineral supplements as well. Without these, especially vitamin D_3 and calcium, day geckos are quite apt to develop a metabolic bone disorder (once simply called "decalcification" or "rubber bone disease"). Rapidly growing young and female geckos that are utilizing calcium to form shells for their developing eggs will be affected more quickly than adult males or nonovulating females. Ideally, the ratio of calcium to phosphorus should be two to one and of vitamin D_3 to vitamin A, one to one. A lack of vitamin D_3 (which enhances calcium metabolism) or an excess of vitamin A can cause skeletal demineralization and deformities.

The use of vitamin and mineral supplements is necessary even with full-spectrum lighting. A formula is suitable for virtually all species of day geckos is given on page 85.

Besides the vitamin-enhanced fruit mixture, day geckos should be given calcium-dusted crickets, waxworms, and an occasional giant mealworm. The size of the insects necessarily varies with the size of the geckos being fed. The 3-inch-long (7.6-cm) yellowheads require fly-sized crickets; the 1-foot-long (30.5-cm) Standing's day geckos relish larger insects.

Reproduction: One of the greatest thrills and challenges for those of us who maintain reptiles is to successfully breed them.

Fortunately, most day geckos respond well to captive conditions. If certain minimum criteria are met or exceeded, many species are rather easily bred.

Depending on the species, day geckos may deposit their clutches in one of two ways: they may be either "egg-gluers" or "non-gluers."
• Egg-gluers: These eggs are often the more difficult to deal with. If the female gecko chooses a side panel or corner of her terrarium on which to glue the eggs, the whole enclosure will need to be kept at the suggested incubation temperature of from 78 to 86°F (25.6–30°C). If the female gecko deposits her eggs on a removable item (flowerpot or plant leaf), then that item can be removed and kept at a proper temperature.

Besides suitable temperature, a high humidity is necessary to successfully incubate gecko eggs (see page 44).
• Non-gluers: The eggs of the non-gluers may be removed from their deposition site to where they are to be incubated. Again, a temperature of from 78 to 86°F (25.6–30°C) and a high humidity are desired.

Incubation media: Either fine vermiculite or sphagnum moss, moistened to a proper consistency and kept at a suitable temperature, is an excellent incubation medium (see page 44).

Incubation duration: Depending on the species of your geckos and the temperature at which the eggs are incubated, the incubation interval will usually be between 6 and 12 weeks.

Incubation temperature: Temperature will determine both the duration of incubation and the sex of your hatchlings. Varying temperatures, from 77 to 85°F (25–29.4°C), will usually produce geckos of both sexes. Eggs incubated at the warmer end of the temperature range usually produce males, those at the cooler end, females (see chart, page 57).

The blue-tailed day gecko is more difficult to breed in captivity than many other species in the genus.

Handling Your Day Gecko: The easiest and most concise instruction I can offer regarding handling day geckos is the single word, "Don't." Don't handle them!

Beautiful though those skins may be, they are remarkably easy to tear. Additionally, a mere bump may cause the tail to autotomize.

Day geckos are alert and fast. They become even more so at the slightest hint of danger. To even long-term captives, an approaching hand equates to grave danger.

If it does become necessary to handle your day geckos, do so firmly but gently. Allowing them to squirm in your grasp will only accentuate the possibility of their skin being torn. Most tears will heal over quickly, and even considerable scars will virtually disappear after several sheds.

GLOSSARY

The terms contained in this section will help define unfamiliar words contained in the text.

Aestivation: a period of warm-weather inactivity, often triggered by excessive heat or drought

Allopatric: not occurring together but often adjacent

Ambient temperature: the temperature of the surrounding environment

Anterior: toward the front

Anus: the external opening of the cloaca; the vent

Arboreal: tree-dwelling

Autotomize: the ability to break easily or voluntarily cast off (and usually to regenerate) a part of the body, such as a tail

Brille: the clear spectacle that protects the eyes of lidless-eyed geckos

Brumation: the reptilian and amphibian equivalent of mammalian hibernation

Caudal: pertaining to the tail

Cloaca: the common chamber into which digestive, urinary, and reproductive systems empty and that itself opens exteriorly through the vent

Gonatodes albogularis notatus is a Hispaniolan yellow-headed gecko.

Con: a prefix indicating "the same" (congeneric refers to species in the same genus)

Crepuscular: active at dusk or dawn

Deposition: the laying of eggs

Deposition site: spot chosen by the female to lay eggs

Dichromatic: two color phases of the same species, often sex-linked

Dimorphic: a difference of form, build, or coloration in the same species; often sex-linked

Diurnal: active in the daytime

Dorsal: pertaining to the back; upper surface

Dorsolateral: pertaining to the upper sides

Dorsum: the upper surface

Endemic: Confined to a region

Endolymphatic sacs: the sacs of calcium carbonate located on both sides of the neck in certain members of the subfamily Gekkoninae

Femoral pores: openings on the underside of the thighs of lizards that produce a waxy exudate

Femur: the part of the leg between the hip and the knee

Form: an identifiable species or subspecies

Fracture planes: weaker areas in the tail vertebrae that allow the tail to break easily

Taylor's fat-tailed gecko, Hemitheconyx taylori, *has proven difficult for breeders to obtain and maintain.*

Genus: a taxonomic classification of a group of species having similar characteristics, falls between the next higher designation of family and the next lower designation of species

Granular: pertaining to small, flat scales

Gravid: the reptilian equivalent of mammalian pregnancy

Gular: pertaining to the throat

Heliothermic: pertaining to a species that basks in the sun to thermoregulate

Hemipenes: the dual copulatory organs of male lizards and snakes

Hybrid: offspring resulting from the breeding of two species

Hydrate: to restore body moisture by drinking or absorption

Insular: island-dwelling

Intergrade: offspring from the breeding of two contiguous subspecies

Juvenile: young or immature

Keel: a ridge (along the center of a scale)

Labial: pertaining to the lips

Lamellae: the transverse scales that extend across the underside of a gecko's toes

Lateral: pertaining to the side

Middorsal: pertaining to the middle of the back

Midventral: pertaining to the center of the abdomen

Monotypic: containing but one type

Nocturnal: active at night

Oviparous: reproducing by means of eggs that hatch after laying

Ovoviviparous: reproducing by shelled or membrane-contained eggs that hatch prior to, or at, deposition

Parietal eye: a sensory organ present in certain reptiles that is positioned mid-cranially

Phalanges: the toe bones

Poikilothermic: a species with no internal body temperature regulation; "cold-blooded"

The Peninsula leaf-toed gecko, **Phyllodactylus nocticolus,** *has widely distended toe tips.*

Posterior: toward the rear

Preanal pores: a series of pores, often in the shape of an anteriorly directed chevron, and located anterior to the anus

Race: a subspecies

Rugose: not smooth; wrinkled or tuberculate

Saxicolous: rock-dwelling

Scansorial: capable of or adapted for climbing

Serrate: sawlike

Setae: the hairlike bristles in the lamellae of a gecko's toes

Spatulae: the flattened distal ends of the setae

Species: a group of similar creatures that produce viable young when breeding

Subcaudal: beneath the tail

Subdigital: beneath the toes

Subspecies: the subdivision of a species; a race that may differ slightly in color, size, scalation, or other criteria

Sympatric: occurring together

Taxonomy: science of classification of plants and animals

Terrestrial: land-dwelling

Thermoregulate: to regulate (body) temperature by choosing a warmer or cooler environment

Thigmothermic: pertaining to a species (often nocturnal) that thermoregulates by being in contact with a preheated surface such as a boulder or tarred road surface

Tubercles: warty protuberances

Tuberculate: pertaining to tubercles

Tympanum: the external eardrum

Vent: the external opening of the cloaca; the anus

Venter: the underside of a creature; the belly

Ventral: pertaining to the undersurface or belly

Ventrolateral: pertaining to the sides of the venter (belly)

Gecko Sources

Geckos that once were rare in the private sector are increasingly available from both private and commercial breeders and importers.

Many sources advertise in the various reptile and amphibian magazines.

Magazines

Reptiles Magazine
P.O. Box 6050
Mission Viejo, California 92690

Web Sites

Important Web addresses:

www.kingsnake.com: the largest and most comprehensive listings of geckos for sale and forums.

www.faunaclassifieds.com: this is another important source for geckos, supplies, and forums.

The beautiful Australian thick-tailed gecko, **Nephrurus (Underwoodisaurus) millii,** *is now considered a knob-tailed gecko.*

Affinity Groups

Herpetological/herpetocultural clubs can be found in many large cities. Check with the biology department of your nearest university or with the personnel of nature centers or museums to find the location of the club nearest you.

Additional Reading

Arnold, E. N., and J. A. Burton. *A Field Guide to the Reptiles and Amphibians of Britain and Europe.* London: Collins, 1978.

Bartlett, R. D. "Phelsuma klemmeri: The Neon Tetra of Geckos." *Reptiles Magazine.* Vol. 1, no. 2, 1993.

_____ "Notes on Standing's Day Gecko." *Tropical Fish Hobbyist Magazine.* Vol. XLII, no. 1, 1993.

_____ *Crested Geckos and Relatives,* Hauppauge, New York: Barron's Educational Series, Inc., 2004.

_____ and Patricia Bartlett. *Leopard and Fat-tailed Geckos,* Hauppauge, New York: Barron's Educational Series, Inc., 1999.

_____ *Day Geckos,* Hauppauge, New York: Barron's Educational Series, Inc., 2001.

Cogger, Harold A. *Reptiles and Amphibians of Australia.* Ithaca, New York: Cornell, 1992.

Conant, Roger, and Joseph T. Collins. *Reptiles and Amphibians, Eastern/Central North America.* Boston, Massachusetts: Houghton Mifflin, 1991.

Frye, Fredric L. *A Practical Guide for Feeding Captive Reptiles.* Melbourne, Florida: Krieger Publishing Co., 1991.

Glaw, F., and M. Vences. *A Field Guide to the Amphibians and Reptiles of Madagascar.* Leverkusen: Moos-Druck, 1992.

Halliday, Tim, and Kraig Adler. *The Encyclopedia of Reptiles and Amphibians.* New York: Facts on File, 1986.

As with many baby geckos, hatchlings of the Madagascar giant day gecko, **Phelsuma madagascariensis grandis,** *are more strongly marked than the adults.*

Jes, Harold. *Lizards in the Terrarium.* Hauppauge, New York: Barron's Educational Series, Inc., 1987.

McKeown, Sean. *The General Care and Maintenance of Day Geckos.* Lakeside, California: Advanced Vivarium Systems, 1993.

Peters, James A. *Dictionary of Herpetology.* New York: Hafner, 1964.

_____ and Roberto Donoso-Barros. *Catalogue of Neotropical, Squamata: Part II. Lizards and Amphisbaenians.* Washington, D.C.: Smithsonian, 1970.

Schwartz, Albert, and Robert W. Henderson. *Amphibians and Reptiles of the West Indies.* Gainesville, Florida: University of Florida Press, 1991.

Slavens, Frank, and Kate Slavens. "Reptiles and Amphibians in Captivity; Breeding, Longevity and Inventory," Current January 1, 1993. Seattle: Slaveware, 1993.

Smith, Hobart M., and Edward H. Taylor. *Herpetology of Mexico.* Ashton, Maryland: Eric Lundberg, 1966.

Stebbins, Robert C. *A Field Guide to Western Reptiles and Amphibians.* Boston, Massachusetts: Houghton Mifflin, 1985.

Wareham, David C. *The Reptile and Amphibian Keeper's Dictionary.* London: Blandford, 1993.

The peacock day gecko, **Phelsuma quadraocellata,** *is inexpensive and beautiful, but can be quarrelsome.*

I N D E X

About the Author

R. D. Bartlett is a herpetologist who has authored or coauthored more than 600 articles and 40 books on reptiles and amphibians. He lectures extensively and has participated in field studies across North and Latin America. In 1978 he began the Reptilian Breeding and Research Institute (RBRI), a private facility. Since its inception, more than 150 species of reptiles and amphibians have been bred at RBRI, some for the first time in the United States under captive conditions. Successes at the RBRI include several endangered species.

Bartlett is a member of numerous herpetological and conservation organizations.

Patricia Bartlett received her B.S. from Colorado State University and became the editor for an outdoor book publisher in St. Petersburg, Florida.

Subsequently, she worked for the science museum in Springfield, Massachusetts, and for the historical museum in Ft. Myers, Florida. She is the author or coauthor of 35 books on natural history and historical subjects.

Acknowledgments

Our thanks to Bill Love (Blue Chameleon Ventures), Rob MacInnes (Glades Herp, Inc.), and Chris McQuade (Gulf Coast Reptiles) for allowing us photographic opportunities. To Tim Tytle, M.D., and Reid Taylor, M.D., our thanks for the many conversations, pointers, and exchanges of ideas. Special thanks to our editor, Pat Hunter for her patience and professionalism and to Fredric Frye, D.V.M., for critically reading and commenting on the original.

Important Note

Geckos may transmit certain infections to humans. Always wash your hands carefully after handling your specimens. And *always* supervise children who wish to observe your geckos.

If you get a scratch or bite from a gecko, be sure to seek prompt medical treatment.

Photo Credits

All photos, including covers, © R. D. Bartlett

Illustration Credits

Michele Earle-Bridges: pages 26, 27; Tom Kerr: pages 44, 45

All inquiries should be addressed to:
Barron's Educational Series, Inc.
250 Wireless Boulevard
Hauppauge, NY 11788
www.barronseduc.com

ISBN-13: 978-0-7641-2855-4
ISBN-10: 0-7641-2855-8

Library of Congress Catalog Card No. 2005050024

Library of Congress Cataloging-in-Publication Data
Bartlett, Richard D., 1938–
    Geckos : facts & advice on care and breeding /
R. D. Bartlett and Patricia P. Bartlett.
        p. cm. — (A Complete pet owner's manual)
        Includes bibliographical references (p.) and index.
        ISBN-13: 978-0-7641-2855-4
        ISBN-10: 0-7641-2855-8
    1. Geckos as pets. 2. Geckos. I. Bartlett, Patricia Pope, 1949– II. Title. III. Series.

SF459.G35B37   2006
639.3'952—dc22   2005050024

Printed in China
9 8 7 6 5 4